—— MISFIT ——
MARKETING FOR
RESTAURANTS

*How to Acquire, Retain,
and Track Guests*

Brett Linkletter and
Jace Kovacevich

TABLE OF CONTENTS

Chapter 1

INTRODUCTION

Misfit Marketing for Restaurants: How to Acquire, Retain, and Track Guests will drastically change the way you approach your restaurant business. If you feel that you have been inadequately served by agencies or are unsure of how to strategically market and grow your business, this book will help you gain clarity in the next steps and long-term planning. By providing comprehensive and applicable knowledge, you will learn how to profitably and predictably scale your business. The principles and content covered in this book will empower you to move forward with confidence.

By using the concepts you learn in this book, you will:

- Start attracting and retaining the best customers for your business

- Be able to track your marketing dollars and gauge if they are bringing you customers in real time

- Grow and scale your business to whatever level you desire

Like with any business, however, it's tough to launch a new initiative or marketing program. When it comes to running a restaurant, owners often have to wear many different hats and manage many different moving pieces operationally. Having a marketing system that you can count on to bring you customers, any time of the year, is incredibly important in securing your long-term success.

With rising payroll, rent, and food costs, you must have predictable revenue streams you can count on, not just to keep your doors open, but to ensure that your business is thriving each and every day!

This book was written for two types of restaurant owners:

- The restaurant owner who is frustrated with current marketing strategies, their marketing agency, or marketing employees, because the results are not meeting expectations
- The restaurant owner who is looking to massively scale and grow their restaurant business, using the most modern and cutting-edge techniques available today

Whether you are struggling to get customers or you're doing well and looking to take your business to the next level, this book will provide you with the insights and information on how to develop the mindset and skills necessary to grow your restaurant through digital marketing strategies.

Throughout this book, we will be sharing real case studies with you. These real results showcase how we have helped our clients achieve success, as a result by adopting the marketing principles outlined in each chapter.

Our goal is not to give you a bunch of theory, but to offer detailed instructions that will provide strategies you can begin implementing today.

Who We Are

We are Brett Linkletter and Jace Kovacevich, founders of Misfit Media, currently the largest restaurant-focused digital-chat marketing agency on the planet. We have worked with over 500 different restaurant concepts internationally, so when it comes to growing a restaurant business through online marketing, we are your resident experts.

Over the past several years, we have helped all kinds of restaurants, from chains with over 100 locations to small mom and pops, and on to fast food, casual dining, and fine dining restaurants. Our niche expertise in this space allows us to continually scale our agency and, along the way, help hundreds of restaurants predictably grow their business and clientele.

How We Started this Venture

We (Brett and Jace) became friends while attending college at the University of Southern California. We first met through our fraternity, Sigma Chi, and immediately bonded. Shortly after graduating, we partnered on Misfit Media and capitalized on the growing need from local and online businesses to help with digital marketing.

In the beginning, we called ourselves a "Full-Scale Digital Marketing Agency for Everyone," which basically meant we did anything and everything for everyone. This was great in theory, but horrible in reality. No one can be everything to everyone.

We worked with every kind of brand and all types of businesses, such as fitness apparel, fitness studios, dental offices, e-commerce, men's and women's fashion, and restaurants. You name it, we tried it. We even tried marketing and selling Botox, which was insane!

Our services included anything you could fit under the umbrella of marketing. We offered social media marketing services, content creation, website development, influencer marketing, SEO (search engine optimization), and app development. We even joked that if a client asked us to move their refrigerator, we would do it! Overall, we were in way over our heads in too many different industries and, in doing so, we were good at everything but not great at anything. At that moment, we knew we had to change our business model and decide what we wanted to focus on.

The secret to success is finding your niche and excelling in that specialty.

Deciding on a niche in the beginning wasn't easy, but after servicing so many industries, we discovered that there was a really, REALLY big problem in the restaurant market.

We decided to hone in on this space.

What was the really big problem?

Restaurant owners couldn't tell whether their marketing was actually profitable!

We witnessed hundreds of restaurant owners throwing money at a variety of different marketing resources, without any idea if any of it was working or if they would earn a profit from any of those resources.

When considering social media marketing strategies, a sign of success in the eyes of many restaurant owners is the number of views, likes, or followers they receive on or from a post. As marketers who have been down this path hundreds of times before, we knew that social engagements do not necessarily mean revenue.

Through our background in a variety of industries, especially the e-commerce brands, we understood the benefits of online data and tracking a definitive return on investment (ROI). With this skill set, we are able to help businesses calculate a defined ROI, track revenue, and scale results to maximize profits.

We realized if we applied some of the strategic marketing principles that we were using on online e-commerce brands to restaurants, we could solve a pretty massive problem in the industry.

Common sense: *The bigger the problem you solve, the more money you can make.*

In 2016, we set out to solve that pain point in the market and solely focus on restaurants. This proved to be the best decision we ever made.

Our First Big Break to Your First Big Break

During the summer of 2016, we had our first big break. We were sitting in a conference room with the owners of one of LA's most famous burger joints. They had 33 locations and were known for their chili burgers and fries. The awesome part about this burger chain is that all of their locations are corporate-owned, meaning that one team makes all decisions across all locations, instead of needing to coordinate with each franchisee. In other words, we only needed to speak to one team to roll out a marketing plan across all thirty-three locations. It was an excellent opportunity for success.

We recognized that this legendary burger concept had been in business for over 60 years and had little to no online strategy at all! Rather than being present online, their marketing strategies were very heavily focused on radio, television, newspapers, and other traditional marketing methods. In fact, they were so old-school that they didn't even have a Facebook page, other than one that a raving fan created and handed over to the company after accumulating thousands of followers.

From the moment we stepped into their business and opened their brand up to the digital frontier, they quickly realized how many online opportunities were available. Within the first three months of working with Misfit, their total sales jumped by 5% year-over-year. We were blown away! The CFO told us that they had never seen a jump in sales like that in their entire 60-year existence as a company.

At that moment, we made a decision to dedicate ourselves to the restaurant space and become the best restaurant marketers the world has ever seen. As a result, we've helped hundreds of restaurants make the transition into the new age of digital marketing, and that's exactly what you'll be learning about by reading this book.

So let's get down to the details of how you can achieve your own new success.

What Our Success Means for Your Success

You are about to embark on a journey to understand what you can do to actually scale your restaurant business.

Most restaurateurs look at their business and marketing efforts from the standpoint that they can only make an impact within their store, one-on-one with customers through "table touches," tasty food, and commendable service. Those strategies work well, but they aren't the end-all to success.

We're about to show you that there are many opportunities to positively impact your customers' experience through online marketing. Customer interaction can begin online and shouldn't end when a customer walks out of your restaurant doors. As a restaurant owner, your interaction with customers can go from digital to physical and back to digital when they leave the restaurant. Digital interaction is where the true magic happens.

We're hoping to eliminate the barriers that currently exist for you in the market and open your eyes to new possibilities that will help you reach customers and create consistent revenue streams for your restaurant.

We break down, in step-by-step detail, how we have profitably grown over 500 restaurant concepts all over the world, using our predictable acquisition and retention systems. You're about to learn exactly how you can grow and scale your restaurant in addition to how to track your customers coming in, down to the dollar. It's going to be a very exciting journey.

We'd like to remind you that the name of our company is Misfit Media.

Misfit is defined as: "a person whose behavior or attitude sets them apart from others in an uncomfortably conspicuous way."

We chose the name Misfit Media because we define ourselves as a company that does things differently. We do things our way, on our own path, and of our own accord. We challenge the norm and refuse to accept the status quo in all aspects of business and life.

Just because everyone's doing something one way doesn't mean it is the right way. We approach business as a band of rebellious misfits, and it's this mindset that has helped us become wildly successful. We believe that if you adopt this "Misfit Mindset," you too, will become more successful.

We love our agency business because it allows us to make a living doing what we love and make an impact on other people's lives, by helping them grow their business. That feels really good.

We are the only agency in the world with two published Facebook case studies that discuss what we've done for restaurants to profitably scale and grow their business with marketing automation via Facebook, Instagram, and Facebook Messenger.

Some of the awards and acknowledgements we've received include winning the "Top Performing Local Business Agency" of 2019 by ManyChat, the largest chat marketing and messenger automation platform in the world.

In addition, our agency has received the ClickFunnels "Two Comma Club Award" for surpassing seven figures in revenue with a single marketing funnel.

At the time of this writing, we've produced over 1,500,000 customer leads for our restaurant partners.

We mention these accomplishments not to brag but to give you confidence that you are learning from the best in the business.

Over the past several years, we've been able to sharpen our skill sets to the point that we have a strong understanding of where the restaurant market is and how the marketing principles we've learned can help any type of business succeed. However, we continue focusing on restaurants because we love this industry and are strong believers that in order to be a true expert, you must focus on one area.

We currently work with restaurants in the United States, Canada, and the United Kingdom, and we are looking into expanding our international customer base.

Chapter 2

APPROACHING MISFIT MARKETING

Adaptability is about the powerful difference between adapting to cope and adapting to win.

Max McKeown

Change is not an option; it is a requirement.

Brett Linkletter

To survive in modern times, a business must constantly adapt. To thrive, a business must embrace the changes in society, culture, and consumer habits.

When it comes to marketing, the biggest mistake restaurant owners typically make is the failure to change the lens of how they view marketing today, as compared to how it was viewed many years ago. We call these restaurant owners the "dinosaurs."

The dinosaurs look at marketing through a macro lens — a perspective that is too open-ended, instead of looking at each strategy or tactic they execute at a micro level, where success can be quantified and analyzed down to the dollar.

Many restaurant owners will say, "When we do television, our sales go up, so this works!" However, what are the long-term effects of this? What other lessons can we gather here? What other aspects influence the rapid jump in sales? Could it be just the time of year that led to these sales, rather than television? And how many of these customers are new versus pre-existing?

The point is that without a micro perspective - on each campaign, you lose necessary data points and valuable feedback you can use to improve ad campaigns and effectively attract more customers.

The next mistake we see many restaurant marketers make, is relying on strategies that aren't backed by numbers. This style of marketing aims to push out as many pieces of social content as possible, in the hope that new customers will see this content and be compelled to visit the restaurant. We call those who pursue these strategies "Hope Marketers." They look at launching marketing campaigns purely from a creative, feel-good perspective and rely on their gut rather than data to make marketing decisions.

The error these Hope Marketers make is concentrating on social media metrics — impressions, views, followers, and likes — instead of tracking actionable data — new customer acquisition, retention, customer lifetime value, etc.

Earning a return on investment (ROI) is always the highest priority in our marketing strategy. At the end of the day, "You can't deposit likes into the bank™," so why would social media likes ever be a metric that you use to determine success?

Ultimately, the biggest issue with hope-based marketing strategies is the lack of evidence to prove they are working. If you can't tell that your marketing is really working, then you simply can't scale it.

Now, we'd now like to take a moment to touch on this word "scale" that gets thrown around a lot.

The term "scale" is often mentioned in the restaurant business without real context in terms of what it actually means. At its core, scaling really means understanding your numbers and being able to create a predictable system that you can increase by a determined multiple in a short time period. Scaling success becomes easier when we retain customer information for remarketing purposes. Without a predictable system to acquire and retain guests, scaling is difficult for many restaurants. We will discuss scaling in more detail in later chapters. However, for now we want to emphasize that the inability to scale due to underdeveloped marketing becomes a massive problem, as a restaurant surpasses a mom-and-pop level.

We recognize that running a restaurant is not an easy task. Marketing is only one component of the restaurant business model, and it's usually an afterthought. It's because of this and the fact that the digital landscape is changing so quickly, that it is incredibly difficult for some restaurants to keep up with emerging digital marketing strategies and tactics.

In this blur of constant change in the marketing landscape, we always keep our clients educated on changes and opportunities that are available. In the course of reading this book, you will gain an understanding and learn how to navigate the ever-evolving world of digital marketing.

Our new strategies and approach to marketing equip our restaurant clients with a new lens, giving them the ability to analyze data with actual dollars and determine the bottom-line success of their marketing with extreme precision.

Knowing these numbers has many other benefits, in addition to tracking profit margins:

- You can scale budgets and make more money, simply by spending more money.
- You have a better handle on projecting revenue months down the line.
- With numbers in hand, you can make some major power moves in deciding when to hire and when to open another location.

This clarity opens your business to additional opportunities.

We know that for every single dollar we spend on marketing for Misfit Media, we have consistently produced an average of $9 in returns over the past two years. With this 9X ROI for every dollar spent, we know down to the dollar what we will be making months in the future for our agency and can predict our own company's growth with precision.

Using this model makes it possible to:

- Generate a steady stream of high-quality guests who keep coming back
- Provide predictable systems around retaining long-term guests
- Track customer spend down to the dollar, so you know exactly what's working

"Knowing your numbers" is one of the many concepts we teach our clients, so they can make better decisions on hiring, expanding their business, and dealing with other facets of running a business.

When it comes to restaurants that already have a decent online audience, oftentimes their extensive efforts still fail to make noticeable changes to their bottom line. By implementing our suggestions, they can create a greater impact with their online marketing strategy.

Most people know that they need to have an online presence — they just don't know exactly what to do. Owners *know* that they need to look good on Yelp, Google, Facebook, Instagram, and even YouTube. The issue is they don't know *how* to properly leverage those platforms to actually generate and track the guests coming in.

Most restaurant owners aren't marketing
on the wrong online platforms;
they are marketing in the wrong way on the right platforms.

When we ask restaurant owners what they are doing to attract new customers, they often reply, "We're on Facebook and Instagram." Just being present on these platforms is not enough to attract new customers.

Additional issues arise when these restaurant owners or marketers aren't able to track the data and communication with customers across these different platforms. For instance, when a customer receives a promotional email from a restaurant, systems need to be in place to track customer activity throughout the campaign. That marketing strategy should record and transmit across their communication channels to prevent that customer from receiving the same promotion again and again.

There are three big issues with the inability to communicate effectively across platforms:

- Advertising dollars are wasted, by repeatedly reaching the same customer with the same message.
- Customers become annoyed by repeatedly seeing the same advertisements.
- Customers who normally pay full price become accustomed to discounted offers.

If you deployed a newspaper ad and launched both a radio and a TV commercial, you may reach a lot of people, but because these different channels aren't integrated — they don't "talk" to each other. You miss opportunities to be more efficient and lucrative with your advertising dollars.

Of course, we've seen big companies like Starbucks and Subway leverage mass media advertising channels to invite customers in, and they are in the top 1% of restaurants in the market. What about the other 99%? That's the gap.

Filling that gap is the purpose of this book — to inform you about the changing landscape of marketing and how our methods can help you increase traffic and revenue at your restaurant.

The Changing Industry

The restaurant space is one of the fastest, most rapidly changing industries on the planet. Just fifteen to twenty years ago, many restaurants had no online presence at all. Today, a good majority of them have more than just an online presence; they have new online distribution channels, which allow them to expand their customer base through delivery. Third-party delivery apps, such as Postmates, Uber Eats, DoorDash, and many others, are completely changing the marketing game.

When you look at consumer behaviors and trends over the last several years, a new market has emerged with people who prefer ordering their food to eat at home versus dining out. People are getting lazier as trends move more toward this on-demand and convenience-based economy. This consumer behavior will continually shift towards the direction of convenience. The restaurant owners who refuse to adapt to these new changes in their business landscape will be left behind, and they will eventually go out of business. On the other hand, those who do adapt to this new change will increasingly benefit from the trends and thrive.

The restaurant success gap will continue to grow, as technology alters the competitive landscape. A big part of your restaurant's success will be determined by your willingness to change.

To meet this growing trend, marketing must follow suit. Unlike traditional marketing — newspaper, radio, television, billboards, etc. — advertising today must progress. What was considered contemporary marketing in recent years — posting photos or videos on social media — is outdated. Unpaid posts only reach a small percentage of your audience, *and* they don't offer statistics that you can track back to customer acquisition.

Digital Marketing — The Omnichannel

The beauty of digital marketing across platforms is that you have the ability to leverage multiple online channels at once to tackle two big objectives — acquiring and retaining customers. We call this style of marketing "omnichannel" marketing.

> *Omnichannel Marketing: A multichannel sales and marketing approach that provides the customer with an integrated experience. Wherever the customer connects with the business — online, by phone, or physically inside the restaurant — the experience is seamless.*

Through modern online technologies, we integrate all involved platforms to create a simple and uniform customer journey.

In other words, our "Omnichannel" experience pulls them in.

As many people may have noticed over the years, organic — or unpaid — reach on social media has plummeted tremendously. Simply posting no longer impacts sales as it once did. Furthermore, posting and getting likes doesn't mean you're earning customers.

In broader terms, traditional marketing is primarily one-sided. Radio advertisements are merely music interruptions. Traditional cable television is fading out, as your customers spend more time on social media and on-demand streaming services, like Netflix. Billboards may catch someone's eye, but it's hard to measure their direct impact on sales. These traditional marketing methods typically don't allow the customer to have much of a conversation with the brand.

People are bombarded with information, and the market is asking for a change, when it comes to communicating with the brands they care about. It's your job as a business owner to recognize this issue and make the change.

In summation, traditional marketing methods don't offer a conversation between the product and the consumer. As marketers, we can't gain clear insight through these old-school channels. We can't tell how the customer feels about a product or a company.

For example, let's just say you paid for your brand to appear on a TV commercial that reached one million people. You might think, "Wow, that'd be great!" Well, would you be able to know exactly how your viewers feel about this commercial? Was it a positive or negative sentiment? Was there something you could have improved? Could you have tested this commercial against other creatives to see what performed better? Would you be able to test for performance at all? If so, what would the performance results look like?

There's no way of knowing exactly what people felt about your commercial or specifically how many guests visited your restaurant because of it.

The unfortunate truth for 99% of brands today, is that attributing customer transactions to a specific advertisement proves to be very tough.

Fortunately, with our new-age style of marketing:

- You can test multiple ads and multiple pieces of marketing in a short timeframe.
- You can determine which ads are producing better results.

With these insights, you can make strategic moves for your business and customers. When you see success, you have the ability to scale that result. More traditional methods don't offer that option nearly as easily as digital platforms.

We understand that some of the points we just brought up will challenge your belief system. Some big restaurant executives will disagree because they have seen considerable success from TV or other traditional styles of marketing. If you've seen success, that's great! What we are discussing here is the new age of marketing, and our goal is simply to show you that there are alternatives with stronger tracking capabilities to older, more traditional advertising methods.

Aside from the internationally known restaurant franchise brands, a large majority of restaurants don't have a huge budget. As a result, they need more of a bootstrap approach to leverage marketing and get a significant return on their investment. This void is what we hope to fill for our clients. We take great pride in the solution we provide.

We categorize digital marketing as marketing that allows businesses to communicate back and forth with customers over different channels, track data over time, track revenue, and gain insight.

Digital marketing techniques allow you to not only produce guests when you want and how you want, but to scale your success. Therefore, when you find something that's working, you can increase your investment, knowing your results will improve proportionally.

Imagine being able to create more money when you want, by simply spending more money. Yes, it sounds crazy, but this is what you can do once you know and understand your advertising metrics and have the right systems in place.

Digital marketing methods also allow you to get the most out of your marketing. Let's say you have a customer that you know consistently enjoys dining at one of your restaurants. Through your data insights on this customer, you can also determine how many times he or she dined with you, what he or she typically spends and what days he or she likes to dine at this restaurant. Ultimately, with this information, you can make smarter decisions in your marketing on how to keep him or her coming back.

Cost Per Acquisition

One of the most important metrics to review in your marketing strategy is your cost per acquisition (CPA). For a marketing strategy to be profitable, the average CPA must be lower than the revenue produced from the average guest.

For instance, if for every $5 you spend on marketing, you produce one dine-in guest who spends on average $50, you earn a $45 profit, excluding food costs, right? If you can continue spending $5 to produce $50, that's a 10X return on your ad investment. Wouldn't you keep doing that all day long, if you could? If you can continue getting this return from your ad spend, you'll eventually scale this up.

Pro tip:

Initially acquiring a guest requires a larger investment than bringing one back.

Using the previous example, you spent $5 to acquire a new guest who will spend $50, on average, on their first visit. Since you also collect the emails and phone numbers of first-time guests, you can track your earned revenue from that initial visit, as well as create a relationship with that guest over their customer lifetime through strategic, low-cost remarketing.

Staying Competitive

The first rule of social media: everything changes all of the time.

As social media becomes more ingrained in our lives, to stay competitive on these platforms, restaurant owners must always be learning and adapting.

Like most aspects of life, continuous learning is very important when it comes to marketing. When we first started our marketing agency, we focused on social media management — producing and scheduling content for Instagram and Facebook. Back in 2015, that simple strategy was fantastic! At the time, it worked fairly well for bringing in new business for our clients.

However, the landscape is now different. If we want to stay competitive and grow, we can't be satisfied with the way things are done today. We need to continuously learn and adapt.

With that knowledge, how do you out-compete the competition online? The answer is simple. You have to be better, stronger, and think with a more data-driven approach.

Additionally, you also have to be more creative! You have to get better click-through rates, and your ads have to be more attractive to your customers. More specifically, you have to be creative in how you reach your customers. We currently love recommending Facebook Messenger to communicate with restaurant customers, because not many businesses are using Messenger in that capacity. Since there are few businesses using this platform the competition is low and the level of consumer interest is extremely high. This is because most businesses haven't yet added Messenger to their marketing strategy.

With so many different platforms online today, how do you know which is best for your business? Before you build your online presence, you need to identify who your ideal customers are and how they engage with your brand. Determining your audience will help you focus your marketing efforts on people who are most likely to become customers. It will also help you understand who your business serves and how to design your marketing strategy to attract more customers.

Analyzing Your Customer Base

Here are some questions to consider:

- How would you describe your ideal customers?
- Would they be eager to engage with you online?
- Would building an online connection between your brand and your customers be meaningful to your customers?
- What online platforms do your customers use the most?
- Do your customers return often?

When choosing which online platforms to focus on, it's also important to understand how people consume content on each platform. For example, if your restaurant is in a tourist area, a platform, such as TripAdvisor or Yelp might be the best platform for you. If your restaurant is in a smaller town that only has a local customer base, using Facebook and Instagram to collect emails and phone numbers as customer leads might be the best route for you.

Are you curious as to how these digital marketing theories work in the real world?

In our introduction, we briefly told the story about the legendary Los Angeles burger chain that we landed as one of our first restaurant clients. Using this new style of customer acquisition, we unleashed a record-breaking campaign for Labor Day weekend.

Case Study: Chili-to-Go

We decided that running ads on Facebook and Instagram was the best strategy to reach the client's ideal customer. It is important to remember that this burger chain hadn't touched any social media advertising prior to working with us. Using Facebook's Ads Manager, we knew we could cast a three-mile radius around each of the thirty-three restaurant locations, targeting locals in the surrounding area. (For those of you not familiar with Facebook Ads Manager, it's Facebook's back-end advertising system that we advise you use to run advertisements.)

We felt good about the vehicle we chose to get in front of customers, but we needed a strategic offer to capture interest. The strategy was to promote a menu item that aligned with the brand and could also reach friends and family of current customers over the Labor Day weekend. In doing so, we believed that this strategy would also boost overall brand awareness to potential new customers.

We decided to run a promotion for chili-to-go for 50% off. Prior to the promotion, this item made up a low percentage of overall sales. However, chili is a staple brand item. Our hypothesis was that it would be well-received, and that the chili would create a strong brand association among new customers. Using proven ad-targeting strategies, we were able to track 600 gallons of chili sold over a three-day period!

Not only did this campaign see a crazy return on ad spend (ROAS) over the three-day period, but we were also able to take a low-selling item and immediately turn it into a top seller, by getting the right offer in front of the right customer. While customers were picking up to-go containers, we were also able to drive an increase of in-store sales. Families were taking those gallons home to barbecues and holiday parties. As a result, this Los Angeles chain was at the center of many dining tables and barbecues and was really reaching an exponential number of new consumers. This is a consumer base that would not have been reached, If we had just done "an" in-store promotion.

Three-Day Weekend Period

Sales : $12,000

Ad Spend : $2,000

Gallons of Chili Sold : 600 (2,400 32-ounce containers)

By thinking creatively and outside the box, we were able to help this client increase transactions on a specific item, while introducing new customers to the brand and building more brand equity within their local community. Not to mention, the time and labor required to actually make, package, and sell the chili was also extremely low, which meant that it was an extremely high profit margin menu item for the brand.

Having their restaurant's brand logo at the center of every barbeque and dining table over that Labor Day weekend also had a long-term effect on sales. The burger chain reported to us that over the next five months, their sales remained 15% higher on this to-go chili item. We attribute 100% of the success in higher sales to our Labor Day promotion, because that promotion exposed this specific item to local customers who had never even known that chili-to-go was an option.

Case Study: Brick Oven Pizza Company

Another case study we'd like to present is from our client, Brick Oven Pizza Company. In this example, we helped another restaurant with an excellent reputation in their local market make the transition from a traditional marketing approach to taking a scientific and data-driven look into attracting new guests to their stores through automation.

This restaurant has fourteen locations, primarily in the Southern and Midwestern regions of the United States. Before working with our agency, they had made several attempts to use social media to generate revenue. However, like many restaurants, they were frustrated and unable to measure whether or not their social media efforts actually attracted new customers.

After many unsuccessful attempts with in-house and agency-run social media campaigns, it's not surprising why many restaurants give up on social media.

In this case, after failing on social media, the restaurant's management decided to go back to word-of-mouth and traditional marketing approaches.

Because Brick Oven Pizza Company had a positive reputation but still had a poor, underdeveloped online strategy, we knew there was a lot of potential to have a major impact with our concept.

They asked us, in a rather frustrated but still hopeful tone, "Well, what makes you guys different?" Fortunately for us, they saw that our agency offered a unique approach to marketing for restaurants. We taught them about our new-age style of marketing, and they took a leap of faith in giving us a chance to help their restaurant succeed online.

Within the first sixty days, we were able to track 2,000+ new customer redemptions, while also collecting 7,600+ email and Messenger subscribers to add to their database.

Yes, you are reading this correctly — 26% of the customers who clicked the ad online actually redeemed at the restaurant! Most restaurateurs who we speak with, are happy to have 20 percent of people open an email, much less obtain them as customers! After struggling for years to get digital marketing to work in their favor, Brick Oven Pizza Company was blown away.

Fast forward to a year later:

We continue to succeed with Brick Oven Pizza Company. We've delivered a 9.5:1 return on their social media advertising spend and tracked over $200,000 in newfound revenue rotating across six locations. We grew their customer database to over 20,000 phone numbers, emails, and Facebook Messenger subscribers.

By taking a step outside of their comfort zone and understanding that they needed a digital strategy in order to continue being successful, Brick Oven Pizza now has a predictable stream of new and returning guests they can count on. In addition, they also now have an ever-growing database of fans, allowing them to create quick momentum at their locations, whenever they want it.

<u>One Year Statistics Over 12 Months at Six Locations</u>

Sales: $257,841

Ad Spend: $27,000

Customer Contacts: 20,525

As you can see, these results from digital marketing techniques are astounding. However, just because we are seeing impressive results from these new methods, doesn't mean we should turn all other marketing efforts off. We mention this because during our initial meetings, our clients often ask, in a concerned and sometimes excited voice, "Should we stop doing our current traditional marketing strategy?"

Here's the thing: if you have a strategy, traditional or otherwise, that you believe is bringing you customers, then by all means you should continue doing it. If something is making you money, why turn it off, right? We recommend that you continue doing what has made you successful in the first place!

On the other hand, if a particular strategy is not making you money, but you still like whatever you're doing, who are we to tell you to stop? Whatever floats your boat!

Our job as a marketing partner is to educate our clients on the opportunities that exist today. Many of the pieces of technology that we now use today to attract top-spending guests were not available, even a couple of years ago.

We are big believers in understanding the WHY behind everything, especially in marketing. Therefore, if our clients are informed and educated on this topic of old versus new marketing, we know they will make the best decision for their business.

There is simply so much online opportunity, both big and small restaurant chains would be remiss if they didn't take advantage of digital marketing and staying omnipresent to customers. This begs the question we answer in the next chapter: *What does it mean to be omnipresent?*

Chapter 3

OMNICHANNEL MARKETING

Rule of 7, Chat Marketing, and Funnels

Have you ever wanted to be in two places at once? Have you ever had to miss your son's football game because you were working late at the restaurant due to an employee calling in sick at the last minute? Have you ever missed an opportunity to capitalize on a last-minute killer deal because you were on a family trip in Mexico? Have you ever wanted to take your restaurant and staff to two different local food festivals to showcase your brand but didn't have a staff large enough to do both at the same time?

Oftentimes, we miss opportunities because we can't be in two places at once.

What if I told you that you could? What if I told you that your brand could communicate with thousands of customers simultaneously, across multiple online channels, and the experience would be seamless?

This multiple channel experience is what happens when your brand is "omnipresent," which is defined as "widely or constantly encountered" or "present everywhere at the same time."

As an agency, we specialize in omnichannel marketing, which we described in chapter one as a multichannel sales and marketing approach that provides the customer with an integrated customer experience. The customer can connect with the business online, by phone, or in person at the restaurant in a seamless experience.

The whole idea behind omnichannel marketing is that you can reach the customer across multiple channels in a customized and scalable manner. To further address this customized manner of marketing, categorize your customers in terms of their level of familiarity with your brand. The way you would address a guest on their first visit to your restaurant is different than a returning, loyal fan, right? Wouldn't you also agree that these same principles should apply in your omnichannel digital marketing strategy? Shouldn't you re-engage with a loyal fan online, just as you greet them again by name when they walk through your restaurant doors? The answer is a strong *yes*.

When omnichannel marketing is set up correctly, you reach new customer prospects who have never heard of your restaurant in a manner that makes sense for a first-time customer. Advertising messages should address the unfamiliar prospect with welcoming copy that introduces your restaurant.

As a prospect becomes more familiar with your restaurant, such as by visiting your website to learn more, remarketing to them should include ads that speak to them with some familiarity.

Whether you are remarketing and re-engaging with a customer using a Facebook ad, Instagram ad, email, or all of these platforms simultaneously (which is the goal of omnipresent marketing), the customer has an integrated experience through our customized marketing approach.

Additionally, with omnichannel marketing in full effect, your brand also appears to be everywhere and, therefore, is always at the top of your target customer's mind.

We understand this may sound complicated and alot to take in, but if you can achieve omnipresence, your brand can literally be in thousands of places, doing thousands of different things at once.

We've moved into a day and age where the customer experience is expected to be the same in-store, online and through delivery. Whether it's an online order, a pickup in-store, or a customer actually dining in, a restaurant should be able to give the customer a consistent and similar experience.

Consider when you buy an Apple product online or in-store — does the messaging and experience seem similar? Do you notice the simplicity in their brand approach in both scenarios? Do you notice the consistency in the brand colors, look, designs, and customer service?

Apple has mastered the customer experience in every way possible. No matter where the customer is and how they are interacting with Apple, the brand experience and messaging is the same.

Be sure that your restaurant is applying these same principles for your brand's channels and across your brand's marketing. In doing so, you will be able to provide better customer service, while also building your brand. This, in turn, allows your brand to be perceived at a much higher value by your customers.

When restaurateurs can't figure out omnichannel marketing, their messaging seems scattered and random. The problem is that many restaurants have a very different look and strategy across their online channels. We may see that their website is outdated with an old logo, their Facebook page is all about an old promotion and their Instagram is about their next holiday party. When it comes to online presence, consistency is key. You must develop a style to use for all channels across the board.

Once your brand style is consistent, your marketing should speak to customers at their personal point in the buying cycle. Your brand's marketing should know what specific relationship it has with the customer it is reaching, and the message should be consistent across all platforms, online and potentially in-store.

To further explain this idea, I want to introduce you to the "The Rule of 7."

Rule of 7

The Rule of 7 is a marketing principle that states your prospects (potential customers) will need to come across your brand at least seven times, before they really notice and start to take action. If this rule holds true, you need your prospects to see you seven+ times to get them to convert into a customer. It takes time for a prospect to build familiarity with a brand. Failure to create these seven touchpoints may result in a weak customer relationship, resulting in the prospect falling out of the customer lifecycle. In marketing, we call this a "leaky bucket."

With the leaky bucket approach, customers can engage and interact with a restaurant from multiple channels, but the "holes" (not retaining customer info and being unable to effectively communicate with their customers) in the restaurant's marketing bucket are drastically reducing their customer retention. The leaks in a restaurant's marketing bucket can harm the restaurant's marketing efforts and confuse or annoy the customer.

Think about what happens when you visit a website to buy something, then you leave and go to another site without making a purchase. What is one of the first things you see online, after you leave the site you were just shopping on? You see the products you were just looking at, and you see them everywhere! With digital marketing, a brand can remarket to a customer who visited their site through Facebook, Instagram, Google, YouTube, etc.

Have you ever had a T-shirt or pair of shoes follow you around the internet? It's because the brand following you has an omnichannel remarketing strategy. They collected your data when you visited their site, recognized that you were interested in their product and now they are attempting to bring you back to their site to complete the purchase. The retargeting ads will usually stop, if you return and purchase the item or if several days pass without a purchase.

As a restaurant marketing agency, we aim to set up similar strategies across our omnichannel campaigns for restaurants. This remarketing approach allows our clients to focus more on customers who actually care and are more likely to buy from them.

What happens when you take omnichannel remarketing and combine it with marketing on a chat platform? The answer is a lethal marketing strategy that will position you in the perfect place for success. However, first, what is "*chat marketing*"?

ManyChat

Chat Marketing

ManyChat, an omnichannel chat marketing software tool, defines chat marketing as: "the process of promoting and selling your products and services through chat apps, including Messenger, SMS, WeChat, and other 1:1 chat apps."

In general terms, chat marketing is marketing that is conversational and allows the business to communicate directly, one-on-one, with customers. Chat marketing creates a dialogue between both parties versus the one-sided marketing that you typically see in traditional methods.

When you take an omnichannel approach to marketing and combine it with chat resources, you are able to connect with the customer in new ways. With omnichannel chat marketing, you can be closer to the customer than ever before. You can engage with customers one-on-one in conversation or through group messaging. You can begin a conversation with a customer whenever you want, or they can begin one with you.

We will discuss chat marketing in more detail in later chapters. When it comes to connecting and building a deep relationship with a customer, there is no better method than chat marketing.

Funnels

At this point, you should understand the concept of omnichannel marketing and how to be present on all platforms. You should also understand the benefits of chat marketing and how you can connect with the customer one-on-one.

How do you apply these concepts together and really take your marketing to the next level? The answer is "marketing funnels."

A marketing funnel is defined as: "a way of breaking down the customer journey all the way from the 'awareness' stage (when they first learn about your business) to the 'purchase' stage (when they're ready to buy your product or service)."

Do you remember previously reading how you want your marketing to engage with a new customer in a certain fashion and a returning customer in another way? This style of marketing, based on level of familiarity, is how funnels work.

The customer journey in your funnel takes a customer from a cold lead, to a warm lead, to a hot prospect, to a guest swiping their credit card at your restaurant for the first time.

A truly effective funnel will bring the customer all the way through that customer journey with specific messaging at each stage, tagged with key performance indicators (KPIs) of success, so you can be accurate in your marketing and remarketing at each step.

As a customer moves through the funnel, their level of familiarity grows. Ads at the top of your marketing funnel are typically meant for new customers, and ads or messages that engage with customers at the bottom of your funnel are typically draws for customers who have actually dined with you. You reengage those customers to invite them to return. Below you will find the general breakdown and steps of a sales funnel.

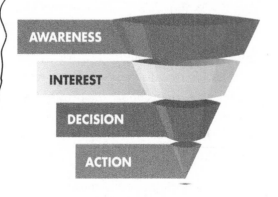

Step 1: Awareness

In the first couple of ads, messages, or points of contact, you want to generate awareness and attract new leads to opt in to your funnel, by clicking, tapping, or writing to you. There are three main entry points that a customer can use to opt in: embedded URLs, social media ads and QR codes. We will discuss each of these in detail in Chapter 5.

Step 2: Interest

The second step is meant to further reel in the customer to capture their contact information. By capturing someone's contact information — their phone number, email, or Facebook Messenger ID — you are getting a stronger buy-in from the lead, which dramatically increases your chances of turning this *potential* customer into a *paying* customer. In addition, you now also have the ability to remarket to this lead for pennies on the dollar. Since your funnels generally capture a first name, last name, email, phone number, and subscription on Messenger, you have multiple channels through which you can re-engage with your customer via your omnichannel marketing.

Step 3: Decision

The third stage aims to push that customer into deciding to visit your restaurant through effective messaging/preselling. During this stage, you send reminders about redeeming an offer, such as a coupon, or perhaps notify the prospect about an upcoming event.

Step 4. Action

The fourth stage is where you see a lead take action and convert to an actual paying customer. From here, since you are able to track a customer visit or an online order in your funnel, you can follow up afterward, sending another offer to generate additional revenue from a repeat visit or order. If not another offer, you also have the option of sending a follow-up survey to get customers' feedback on their experience.

There is a reason why this four-stage process is called a funnel. A funnel is shaped with a large opening at the top and a small opening at the bottom. As you move customers from the top to the bottom of your funnel, you will always see audience engagement drop off. You expect a significant drop at each stage of your funnel, but the trick is to keep the drop off as small as possible!

What we've just explored in marketing funnels is a common practice among almost every major brand currently on the market.

We use funnels in our agency, and it's been the reason we have had a consistent line of restaurants signing up for our marketing services every day for the past several years. Our marketing funnel allows us to create or slow demand for our business, simply by increasing or decreasing our ad budget. This funnel system allows us to go years without having to place cold calls, send cold emails, or knock on doors to get new business. Our marketing funnel is the reason for our rapid growth. We apply the same principles to each and every one of our restaurant clients to help them to also produce customers.

"Understanding marketing funnels means understanding how to produce customers." Funneling is a lever.

This chapter was about taking an omnichannel approach to your marketing and figuring out how to stay in front of customers who have the highest likelihood of visiting your restaurant.

To help paint a clear picture of how to effectively implement an omnichannel strategy, we want to give a few specific examples of how a growing Texas ice cream franchise applied this marketing strategy on a limited budget.

Case Study: The Grand Opening

When we first began to work with this client, they were about to open their third location. However, they were struggling to enter a new market, where no one knew they existed.

This ice cream client wanted to partner with the Misfit Media team to help them get in front of local customers and drive a successful grand opening campaign on a limited budget. Most of our clients have difficulties with grand openings prior to attaining our help. Unless a restaurant is backed by a big corporate budget, they "typically" may only have a couple thousand dollars available to draw as much hype as possible around the new location.

In the case of the ice cream shop, the franchisee had two successful locations. However, the new location outside of Dallas was a new territory. The owner planned to invest everything he had in this third location, with the hope that it would take off like the first two locations. He was putting all his trust in us, and we had to make this campaign work.

After doing a competitive analysis, we decided that running Facebook ads to an event page would be their best option. We attracted and educated registrants about the event through video content and long-form sales copy in the ads. Once Facebook users engaged with the ads or the event page, we were able retarget those users with a series of ads leading up to the event. We sent people who registered for the event a new photo or video ad on Facebook and Instagram each day, starting five days before the grand opening. These customers saw the franchise brand every day with a new message, creating multiple touch points, thus building trust with the franchise brand.

To entice people to attend the event, we created a window between noon and 2:00 p.m. for guests to show up for free ice cream. Giving restricted time frames creates a sense of urgency, especially with grand opening campaigns.

Curious about what happened? Here's a picture of the line that wrapped around the building:

Budget: $2,000

Event Registrants: 1,800

Cost Per Registrant: $1.11

Attendees: 558

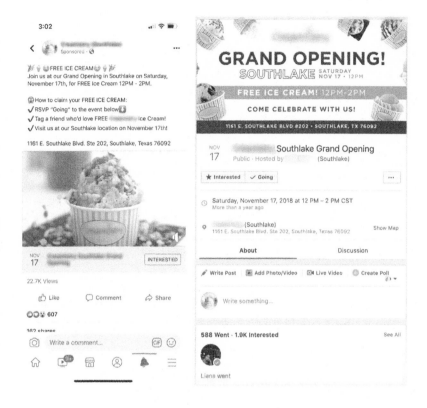

The event was a major success. Using Facebook and Instagram ads along with Facebook events, we collected a list of interested customers for future remarketing and had 558 customers from our campaign show up to the grand opening!

Chapter 4

OWN YOUR DATABASE

Just having satisfied customers isn't good enough. If you really want a booming business, you have to create raving fans.

Ken Blanchard

The cost of acquiring new customers and maintaining those relationships in an online environment versus bricks and mortar is significant.

Stephen Cohen

To acquire customers online and turn them into raving fans that keep coming back, you need to:

- Serve mouth-watering food and offer a fantastic service
- Consistently re-engage with these customers to keep them thinking of you, talking about you, and returning to the restaurant

> Your bottom-line objective is to create a database of customers who know you, like you, and trust you. The database will allow you to apply modern digital marketing methods through Facebook Messenger and text messages to continually re-engage the customer.

But let's not get ahead of ourselves. We will take this in two steps:

- First, we will discuss how to build your customer database.
- Second, with a database in hand, we will delve into making customer-winning ads.

Customer Database

A customer database is the collection of information that is gathered from each of your guests. The database includes contact information, such as a person's name, address, phone number and email address. Your database can also include more detailed information, like the lifetime value of the customer, their purchase history and so forth. Acquiring a following on social media or users in your own app could also be considered a database.

Regardless of the industry, having a strong and active customer database is the most important asset for any marketing strategy.

To preface this process, let's dive into a quick history of social media to explore the power of list building and why building a social following isn't quite enough today.

We all witnessed the power of databases as social media rose in popularity. Brands that built large followings on Instagram, Facebook, YouTube, Twitter, or other social media sites typically beat out their competitors and succeeded in their respective businesses.

A strong following on social media was an indicator of a successful business.

Social media opened up people's minds to the power of garnering an audience of leads, customers, and fans.

However, something happened that changed the game of social media forever: the rulers of social media, Facebook, changed their newsfeed from reverse chronological to algorithmic. Reverse chronological newsfeeds show users content based on when it was posted, with the latest posts at the top of the newsfeed. For example, let's say you followed two people named John and Lisa. John posted a photo on Saturday morning and Lisa posted a photo on Saturday afternoon. You then check your newsfeed on Sunday morning. A reverse chronological newsfeed will show you Lisa's post and then John's, since Lisa's post was more recent.

Algorithmic newsfeeds show users content based on their digital habits — accounts they interact with, tags they use and post popularity, to give a few examples. Algorithmic newsfeeds aim to predict the content that users want to see. Continuing with the above example, if your newsfeed is algorithmic, John's photo may come up first, if it received more engagements than Lisa's or for a variety of other reasons entirely. Reverse chronological newsfeeds display content based on the timing, while algorithmic newsfeeds display content based on user behavior patterns.

Changing how content is featured drastically affects what users see. Before algorithmic feeds, users saw whatever posts were most current from those whom they followed. With algorithmic newsfeeds, users are at the mercy of seeing whatever Facebook's algorithm deems most relevant. This makes it increasingly difficult for brands to recapture their audiences' attention. Surprisingly enough, Facebook does allow its users, as of now, to change their newsfeed settings to reverse chronological order, if desired. However, most users don't know about this setting and stick to their algorithmic newsfeed.

The biggest difference between these newsfeed structures, is that users are much less likely to see posts from accounts they follow, especially from business accounts. With the changes in full effect, brands quickly saw a drop in their engagement, shares, activity, and overall reach. With this drop in social engagement came a drop in earnings and profits.

You may be thinking to yourself, "Why would Facebook do this?" The answer is to boost Facebook's revenue through increasing customer engagement and ad revenue.

Facebook's job is twofold:

1. Keep users entertained on their platform.
2. Make money.

Facebook wants the content on its feeds to entertain its users and keep those users on the platforms as long as possible. Facebook also knows its power and impact to help brands gain attention from users. What did they do to appease their users, while still maximizing their revenue? They prioritized content from users' "friends, family, and groups" and pushed all brand content to the bottom. To be visible on the feed, brands now needed to buy advertising space from Facebook to get their content in front of their customer base again.

We bring up this short history lesson to make a point that when building your database, it's important to OWN it. Brands that build their followings (or database) through social media don't actually own the data from those leads; the social media site does. It only took one day for Facebook to suddenly implement a change that caused millions of brands to suffer monetarily, because of lost leads and reach.

As you go about building your database, you *must* have a way to *own* your leads. The only true pieces of customer contact information that are owned are phone numbers and emails, since these assets connect you directly to a customer, versus relying on another social platform that can change its rules at any given moment.

The Importance of a Database

We will begin by stressing again the importance of developing a customer database.

Your database is *the* most important asset in your marketing strategy.

Building a customer database is the first step in building a successful marketing funnel. Imagine trying to build a relationship with anyone, without the ability to call or text them. Sure, you may run into this individual from time to time and slowly build a relationship. However, with a piece of contact info, you can accelerate the relationship to a deeper level, you can reach out whenever you want, and you can gain more control of your interactions. It's close to impossible to build a relationship with a customer without being able to reconnect with them.

As we addressed in the last chapter, with the Rule of 7, it takes an average of seven touch points to earn a customer's business. Recognizing this rule, if you can contact a lead at almost zero expense through an email or text, your cost to convert this lead into a customer decreases dramatically.

Let's explore this concept with a traditional versus digital marketing scenario for acquiring a new customer.

With traditional marketing (print, billboards, radio, TV), it's nearly impossible to collect any information on your customer.

In a direct hypothetical comparison between traditional and modern digital strategies, let's say you run a traditional campaign with a billboard and a radio segment offering a buy-one-get-one deal to anyone who comes into the restaurant and mentions the billboard or radio ad for the next month. In this campaign, you spend $3,000 with the goal of acquiring new customers.

At the end of the month, you see that you acquired 300 new customers, after tallying up all the BOGO deals that were redeemed by customers. This gives you a cost per customer acquisition of $10, excluding food costs ($3,000/300 = $10/acquisition). Overall, it would be a pretty killer scenario!

However, let's compare what could happen with a more modern style of digital marketing, where you collect each lead's contact information and incorporate the strategy of building a database.

In this example, you again spend $3,000 to acquire new customers in the surrounding area. However, this time, you run ads on Facebook and Instagram, targeting people within a three-mile radius of your restaurant. You ask for their name, phone number, and email in exchange for a coupon for a buy-one-get-one deal.

At the end of the month, with the $3,000 you spent, you acquired 300 new customers, just as you did in the traditional campaign.

However, with this $3,000 spent on social ads, you also acquired 3,000 phone numbers and emails from your new customers.

In the following month, you simply send out an email and text message blast to the remaining 2,700 customers who never came in that first month. At the end of month two, you've acquired another 300 new customers who came in to redeem your BOGO deal, bringing your new customer total to 600.

Over time, as you continue engaging with your list, you may see more and more customers come through your doors, increasing your overall customer base and giving you a better ROI over time from the original $3,000 investment. With your new database of customers, you can also re-engage with these customers as they visit you, thus increasing repeat visits.

When we put the two together and compare traditional to digital strategies that include a database, it's difficult to justify using traditional marketing strategies over digital tactics. The use of a database and the ability to re-engage with your customer base is much too powerful to ignore.

Chapter 5

CONVERTING LEADS INTO CUSTOMERS

As important as it is to build a customer database, you must understand that simply asking leads for their contact info is not a guarantee that they will join your list. After all, a phone number is one of the most personal pieces of contact information to hand over to a company.

To collect your customers' info, you need to make a trade with them! You give the potential customer an offer, if they share their contact information. This is exactly what we did in the scenario in Chapter 4 — using digital marketing techniques, we gave a buy-one-get-one (BOGO) deal in exchange for a lead's contact information.

Collecting Your Lead's Contact Information

A customer database is a powerful asset for any business, but how do you go about capturing this information? After working with hundreds of restaurants across the world, we've been exposed to and implemented a number of different strategies and techniques for a growing customer database.

An old-school strategy for acquiring customer leads' information would be handing out a form at the end of a meal at your restaurant asking for an email or phone number. Another old-school strategy would be to create a contest at your restaurant where customers can throw business cards into a bucket with the chance of winning something. A more contemporary idea might be to have an email capture form on your website that asks customers to join your mailing list.

While these strategies do collect customer information, they are inefficient and outdated. We encourage you to be forward-thinking and address more effective digital strategies. Let's break this down.

As we mentioned, we suggest that you collect the following pieces of information from each customer:

- First and last name
- Email address
- Phone number
- Subscription to Facebook Messenger

The way to capture that information is now fairly easy and far more effective than traditional tactics. We use website advertisements, links embedded in emails, and QR codes that customers can scan with their phones. We will go through how each of these work. However, keep in mind that this is merely the first step for your real goal — sending promotions directly to prospective customers whenever we want, with enticing offers that require no effort on their part, other than glancing at their cell phones.

How to Gather Names and Contact Information to Build a Database

As mentioned in Chapter 3, the first step to collecting customer data is attracting viewers to click on an "entry point" to your marketing funnel. An entry point is the point at which a prospective customer will first engage with marketing assets from the business. In order to get prospective customers to click on an entry point, we also need to give them a reason or incentive to do so, which is why we like to utilize offers.

The three main entry points we typically recommend are:

- Website URLs
- Social media ads
- QR codes

Once a customer enters your marketing funnel for an offer, the best way to capture their information is by using chat automation or a chatbot on Messenger. Utilizing chat automation allows you to capture information from a customer, just like you might use a lead form on a website to capture information. The biggest difference between the two is in the process of *how* you capture a customer's information. If you use a form, a customer simply fills out a number of cells with their information. In chat automation, through a conversational format, you can ask for each piece of information one by one. This allows you to create a more natural and intimate experience overall for the prospect.

In order to chat with your customers through Messenger and ultimately collect their contact information, you first need them to "opt in" or click into a conversation with you, usually in exchange for an offer or promotion.

We will now discuss how you can use each of these three entry points in combination with Facebook Messenger to collect leads information.

Entering a Messenger Funnel from a Website URL

To build a URL entry point, you will need to create a web link that connects directly to your Messenger funnel. A URL is a website address that can be placed anywhere online. Once you create your link, you can embed it on a button on your site, place it in the bio section of your Instagram or Facebook page, or add it to the end of a blog post. This URL entry point is extremely flexible and can be placed virtually anywhere. However, don't forget to give your prospects a reason or incentive to click or tap on your link! Users simply click or tap your link and automatically enter your Messenger funnel. From there, your Messenger chatbot will capture all of the necessary information.

Entering a Messenger Funnel from an Online Ad

The second way to build an entry point is through an online ad. You can do so by creating an ad on Facebook, Instagram, or another platform. The idea here is to link your Messenger funnel to the ad, so when potential customers click your ad, they are directed into your funnel. Once in the funnel, your automated chat sequence will capture the customer's contact information.

If your goal is to increase the size of your customer base, it is important to run ads that target new (cold) audiences, or audiences that are unfamiliar with your restaurant. To capture the attention and contact information of this unfamiliar audience, we typically recommend promoting an aggressive offer on your ad, since the audience targeted is less familiar with or not familiar at all with your brand. Try putting yourself in the viewers' shoes — why would you give some random business you've never heard of your personal contact information? Your promotion must be very enticing!

We highly recommend doing high-ticket offers — our favorite offer is a buy-one-get-one deal. BOGOs are a useful strategy because they are very intriguing, don't break the bank and are often redeemed by groups of friends, rather than one single person. If we can get two people to come in for the price of one, that gives the restaurant more opportunities to delight a greater number of customers and expose more people to the restaurant.

We want to make one thing clear: Running a BOGO deal will NOT turn your restaurant into a discount brand. When you run an ad to a complete stranger online, consider it a trade in order to acquire that person's information. Yes, offering discounted food does add a cost to your overall campaign spend. However, you now "own" that customer's information and have the ability to generate repeat business from them in the coming months and even years. The long-term benefits significantly outweigh the upfront costs to acquire that customer's information.

Messenger Funnel from a QR Code:

A QR code is a unique, computer-generated code that stores web addresses (among other things) and can be scanned and read by a smartphone. Users can simply aim their phone's camera at the code and are then redirected to a predetermined link. Think of it as a square barcode or a hyperlink in the physical world. They are completely customizable and can be accessed by anyone with a smartphone. For example, you could set up a QR that could trigger sending a text, collecting a phone number, downloading an app and so forth. The options are really endless.

Example QR code:

A QR code is another resource for getting customers to opt-in to your Messenger funnel for an in-person interaction but again don't forget to give prospects a reason to scan your QR code!

This particular QR code will send you a message inside Facebook Messenger. Scan it with your phone's camera to view how this QR code captures contact information through Messenger in live time!

QR codes have been around for years but have just started gaining real popularity as of early 2020. Until late 2019, users needed a special app in order to scan a QR code. Today, most up-to-date iPhones and Android phones can scan a QR code with their native camera apps.

QR codes have been very interesting for us, as we have seen them growing in popularity and customer adoption. With all the in-person traffic coming into a restaurant, it's a ready resource for capturing contact information!

How do you create a QR code? You can generate them from a number of different software programs. Our preferred software is ManyChat. It has a slick user interface, and it easily integrates with other applications, like text, email, and Facebook Messenger. To be clear, when the code is scanned by a prospect, you do not automatically get a prospect's name, email, and phone number. Instead, it will take the prospect through the Messenger funnel you created, just the same as when using a URL or ad entry point.

You should display the code in a variety of places, so customers can scan it at your restaurant. We recommend printing it on your menu, creating a window sticker, making a poster for front-of-house, and even printing it onto individual table tents. The goal is to get the code in front of as many customers as possible, so it has the best chance of getting scanned by the maximum number of customers.

Other creative strategies you can try include printing QR codes on bags and to-go boxes and making stickers and placing them anywhere people are likely to see and scan them. For quick service restaurants (QSR)s, we've also seen companies put the QR code on the screens of their customer-facing point of sale (POS).

QR codes are most commonly placed in-store or on product packaging. Therefore, those who scan QR codes are usually existing customers. We know that restaurants don't like making offers to existing fans, but you still need to provide an incentive to capture a customer's contact information. Either a free drink offer or free appetizer should do the trick to reel in a customer for a repeat purchase. If they like your restaurant, they should opt-in fairly easily with a small offer.

Opt-In Overview

By having all three opt-in channels (URLs, ads, and QR codes), you are able to capture leads from almost all angles. Over time, you will see the compounding benefit this information provides.

The value of your initial opt-in offers will depend on how familiar your audience is with your brand.

Case Study: Ice Cream Franchise

To give you a real example so you can see these list-building tactics in full effect, we wanted to bring back our experience with a growing ice cream franchise. Once the franchise owner had his third location up and running, we knew it was time to really put our foot on the gas pedal and start creating a steady stream of customers for their three locations. If you are an experienced restaurant owner, you know the best way to earn new loyal guests at your restaurant (or in this case, ice cream shop) is to first get them into your store to try your product!

For this franchise client, we were working with tight margins. In addition, we had $750/month to work with for a marketing budget. Once again, we found ourselves in a position in which we had to figure out a way to make a strong ROI with a small marketing budget.

Because this chain is known for its ice cream and shakes, we put out a buy-one-get-one-free ice cream or shake offer to invite *new* guests to the shop. Similar to the grand opening, we used Facebook Ads Manager to map out every customer touch point. We used existing content from their Facebook and Instagram pages that already had a high amount of organic engagement to create the ads. (Social media posts with high levels of non-paid social interaction will often translate to a high-performing ad.) This campaign's objective was "message." This feature allows you to link your ads directly to your Facebook Messenger funnel, where you can continue a one-on-one chat experience with potential customers.

In their first sixty days, we sent their three locations over 1,300 customers, while only spending $1,500 on ads. We drove their customer acquisition cost down to just over $1. Boom!

First 60 Days for 3 Ice Cream Locations

> Budget: $1,500
>
> Redemptions: 1,358
>
> Cost Per Acquisition: $1.10
>
> Sales: $13,496

Think about your average check value. Is it $10? $15? Maybe you are a sit-down style restaurant, and it's closer to $50. Whatever that value is, $1.10 to get a new customer through the doors is a steal. Are you starting to see the potential of making money by spending money on ads?

We hope these case studies are opening your eyes to what is possible.

Chapter 6

CHAT MARKETING

Using Email, SMS, and Facebook Messenger to Engage Customers

As mentioned in the previous chapter, the goal for every campaign is to capture a prospective customer's email and phone number and have them subscribe to your Facebook Messenger channel. Text message, email, and Facebook Messenger are the three primary channels that we focus on, when we refer to a database. While social media followers can be useful, we don't place much focus on them because of the continuous reduction of organic reach. Social media followers are becoming less and less relevant each year, and that trend is not changing anytime soon.

Before you engage with your customer database, consider how people communicate on each platform. As we mentioned in Chapter 3, your brand's voice should be the same across multiple platforms or channels. However, it is important to understand that each channel may contain different written copy or designs to reflect the style of the channel you are using. It is important to construct your messaging specifically for each channel and device.

For example, you wouldn't send a a long email newsletter with a big graphic in the same way you would send an SMS text. If you did decide to do this, it might come off as awkward or uncomfortable. The graphic that looks clean in an email format may look out of place inside an SMS text. This is why it's essential to tailor your messages differently for email, text, and Messenger.

The more information you can gather from customers, the faster you can build a relationship with them and the easier it is to stay in front of them. You also want to communicate with customers in the way that is most convenient for them. This will help maximize your open rates, engagement, and sales. For example, if someone doesn't want you to text them, you can send them an email. If someone doesn't have Facebook Messenger on their phone, you can send them a text. People's contact information can also change over time. For instance, the primary email that you use now may be different than the one you used five years ago.

Having a database means nothing, if you don't know how to communicate seamlessly across each platform. In order to do this successfully, you need to understand how one platform differs from another. In addition, you also have to understand the interconnected relationship between all of them. Most restaurant owners have heard of or currently use text, email, and Facebook Messenger, but few weave all three together to create an omnichannel experience.

This chapter will teach you the secret of how you can weave together texting, email, and Facebook Messenger.

The beauty of collecting these three pieces of customer information in every marketing campaign is the ability to diversify communication and create multiple touch points with customers. Before we break down how to communicate across platforms, we want to first explain each platform individually, their pros and cons and why it's beneficial to use all three.

Email

Of the three critical pieces of information, email marketing has been around the longest. When capturing customer email information, we experience the lowest amount of resistance, meaning people are comfortable giving away this information. Once you have a list of emails gathered, there are hundreds of platforms you can use to message your list as often as you like. Let's go over the pros and cons of email marketing.

Pros:

- Easy to capture — Most prospects are more willing to give away their email than a phone number or another piece of contact.

- Ease of use — There are many software platforms today that allow you to construct emails with beautiful templates and styles.

- Low message cost — It is usually cheap to send emails to a large list of contacts and host the list.

- Restrictions — There are no restrictions on how often you can email your list.

- Long-form content — Email is an ideal platform to deliver complex information that needs more explanation than you'd put in a text.

Cons:

- Low open and reach percentage — Even if you have an extensive list of customers, only a small percentage is likely to open the email, and even fewer will actually click on the email content. In 2019, the average email open and click-through rate (CTR) for the restaurant industry was 19.77% and 1.34% respectively.

  https://mailchimp.com/resources/email-marketing-benchmarks/

- Unreliable contact point — People can give a fake or junk email address.

- Automatic flagging — Email hosting platforms now use filtration processes, which can land your email into a section where it will never be opened. For example, Gmail now has a "promotions" tab that can mark your email as junk.

To get around automatic flagging, prompt your readers to engage or respond to the email. Place a call to action button ("Click Here to Get Your Offer") within the email or prompt the customer to respond to claim the offer ("To reserve your table, please respond to this email with the number of people who will be joining you").

Email is still extremely valuable and serves as an effective entry point into other chat marketing applications. An email can also convey a great deal more from a branding perspective with more design capability.

Lastly, everyone has an email address. Therefore, it is still seen as a universal channel that people use to communicate on a daily basis.

SMS

Text messaging is the most mass-adopted form of digital communication. Some people have five different email addresses, but people rarely change their mobile phone number. If you can capture a legitimate phone number, there is a high probability that you can reach that person now and in the future.

Pros:

- High open rate — 98% of texts get read.
- Numbers rarely change — People generally do not change their cell phone number.
- It's concise — The limited number of characters forces the message to be short and sweet.
- It's conversational — People are used to communicating daily through text. It feels personal and social.

Cons:

- Harder to capture — People typically tend to be more resistant to giving away their phone number.
- Relatively expensive — SMS marketing platforms work on a cost-per-message basis. Prices can range from $.075 to $.04 per text message. Messaging a list of 10,000 customers costs between $100–$400.

Messenger Apps — Facebook Messenger

By definition, texting and messaging apps appear similar because both create a one-on-one chat experience, but there are some major differences. For anyone born before the mid-1990s, do you remember your first AIM (AOL Instant Messenger) screen name? It's funny to think about, but this was one of the first breakthroughs with messaging communication.

Instant messaging is real-time, online chat enabled through an online software application. Many of the third-party applications that enable messaging have robust features that also enable file sharing, video chat, and voice calling. Some of the most popular messaging applications in the United States include: Facebook Messenger, WhatsApp, Snapchat, and Skype.

In the restaurant marketing space, Facebook Messenger is the most successful with 1.3 billion active global users. Because Facebook Messenger has already been adopted by so many people world-wide and is used by them on a daily basis, it is a highly effective way to communicate with customers.

Pros:

 Easy to capture — Connects directly to Facebook and Instagram user profiles.

- Automated — Creates a unique, one-on-one conversation with zero to little human effort and attention.

- High open and click-through rates — Facebook Messenger currently sees open rates of 80–90% and CTR of 45–50% on Messenger broadcasts.

Cons:

- Volatile — The rules around Messenger subscribers are ultimately controlled by Facebook and are subject to rule changes at any time.
- Higher level of skill needed — To properly leverage Facebook Messenger, third-party software like ManyChat or Chatfuel are necessary. These platforms come with a learning curve.

Later in this book, we'll show you some examples of Facebook Messenger in action and how we use it in various ways for our restaurant clients.

How to Communicate Across All Three

Now that you have a strong understanding of the three biggest communication platforms in the market, it's important to understand how to communicate across all three.

When you look at Chat marketing at its core, is a two-way conversation. If you think about a conversation that you would have with a friend through text, your friend wouldn't send paragraphs of information. Instead, they would say something like, "Hey, what's up?" As a best practice with any form of chat marketing, we recommend keeping messages concise and conversational. This creates high-quality, efficient conversations between the restaurant and guest.

Below, on the left, you will see an example of high-quality conversation through chat marketing. As you can see, it is short and straight-to-the-point.

Below, on the right, you will see an example of an incorrect way to engage in chat marketing. Don't let your chat conversations turn into a short novel stuffed into a text message box. When in doubt, keep your messages short and ask questions that are most relevant to the consumer.

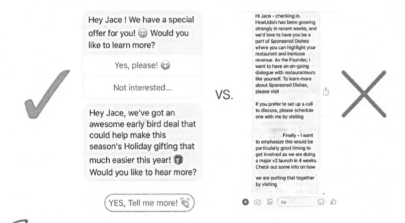

When it comes to effectively communicating with your database, the goal is always to move customers into a one-on-one chat experience. Doing this will build more meaningful relationships quickly with existing and potential guests. You also have unique capabilities inside Facebook Messenger, like sending videos, capturing a guest's check amount, giving directions to a restaurant, and pre-populated reply buttons (shown in the image above) to aid this process. These functions can also be replicated in SMS conversation but they can be costly. SMS capabilities for delivering information are limited, compared to Facebook Messenger.

You may be wondering why we don't just message people through Facebook Messenger, if it has the best chat experience. As mentioned, when outlining the different communication channels above, Facebook Messenger has unlimited potential, but it is regulated with rules implemented by Facebook. Specifically, Facebook allows users to send an unlimited number of messages to their database for free, *if* the conversations happen within a 24-hour window.

To keep the integrity of the platform high, Facebook only allows businesses to send messages to their subscribers who have previously replied to a message within the last 24 hours. Facebook does this to maintain control of the user experience. It limits advertisers from spamming subscribers with unwanted content.

To keep the conversation going (and to keep access to the customer), we use other customer pieces of information (like a phone number and email address) as entry points back into Messenger to restart the conversation.

If we can get restaurant guests to engage with an email or click on a link in a text message, we restart Facebook's 24-hour rule and can message guests for free. This approach to chat marketing creates a uniform message across all platforms and appears everywhere to prospects, leading to an omnichannel experience.

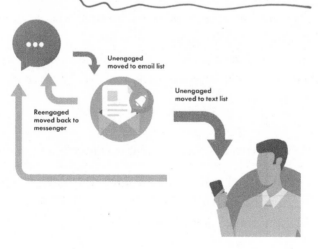

Unengaged moved to email list

Unengaged moved to text list

Reengaged moved back to messenger

In the graphic, we see the intention of all email and text messages is to drive customers back into Messenger to continue a one-on-one chat conversation. With any given campaign, if you can reach customers through email and text, as well as get the prospect to chat with you back and forth through Messenger, you turn one interaction into ten, reaching that customer on multiple applications.

Now, look back at Chapter 3 on Omnichannel Marketing, where we discussed the Rule of 7. We know that your prospects generally need to come across your brand at least seven times, before they really notice and take action. This helps them remember you amid an overwhelming amount of marketing messages and other information, and it positions you to get better results from your marketing efforts.

For example, if someone sees a billboard, that's one touch point. If someone receives an email after, that's another. The reason so many restaurants have trouble getting results from their marketing campaigns, is that they typically reach customers once or twice and then they stop. If a customer is having a back-and-forth conversation with your brand through a messaging channel like Facebook Messenger, you're building that relationship at a rapid rate. Every back-and-forth conversation creates additional points of communication. As a result, you earn customers through chat marketing.

Chat marketing campaigns can create the seven needed touch points to win a customer, all within one conversation!

To execute this multi-channel messaging, there are a number of software programs that a restaurant can use to take action and start executing this immediately. One platform that we recommend is

ManyChat. It helps to create an omnichannel experience across all platforms, delivering the email, SMS, and Facebook Messenger messages in a strategic order.

Case Study: Miller's Roast Beef

When it comes to the proper use of a database to drive consistent business, Miller's Roast Beef stands out as a prime example. One of the most rewarding parts about our job is helping businesses, like Miller's, discover what type of results are available using digital marketing. We actually have an official case study published by Facebook highlighting our success with Miller's Roast Beef.

You can check it out in the link below.

https://www.facebook.com/business/success/millers-roast-beef

As we mentioned, many restaurants (most businesses for that matter) neglect the importance of building a database. Honestly, we don't blame them. Most customer loyalty systems and software for collecting customer information lack the ability to provide a solution to turn those prospects into paying customers.

While you may be able to collect emails in exchange for wi-fi access (companies like Zenreach are popular for this), you aren't creating a relationship with those customers. Such systems are better at capturing the data, rather than providing a solution to properly leverage the data itself. These systems are not sales focused. If you have a ton of emails and phone numbers but don't know what to do with them, what's the point?

Miller's Roast Beef saw such huge success because of their commitment to list building and owning their customers. When Miller's first approached us, their business relied solely on word-of-mouth marketing, and they were ready for a change.

We want to make it clear where we stand with traditional word-of-mouth marketing for restaurants. We are not saying delicious food, amazing service, and a strong connection with the local community isn't important. It is 100% needed. You need to perfect all of those aspects of your business, before any marketing can take place. However, a digital marketing plan on top of an established, positive reputation can help take a restaurant to the next level.

Although Miller's was having success, they needed a digital strategy to bring new guests through the doors. We also provided Miller's with a tracking system, so they could accurately measure the success of their marketing campaigns. If you can't make a direct connection from your marketing efforts to your revenue, you have no idea if those efforts are even working.

Within the first couple of months of working together, we were able to supercharge their email and Facebook Messenger database with thousands of prospective customers. With this new weapon of interested customers at our fingertips, we wanted to generate a boom in sales across their two locations. Using Facebook Messenger, we were able to engage with their customer base in a cost-effective and enticing way: offering a buy-one-get-one-free deal for Miller's signature roast beef sandwich. The offer had a week-long window, which we were hopeful would result in a surge of sales.

We were amazed by the results! The campaign drove in 417 additional purchases over the course of a week, which resulted in $7,000 of newfound revenue. All of this was done on $0 of ad spend. Miller's dedication to building their customer database made this campaign wildly successful.

Miller's continues to engage with this database on a monthly basis to create additional revenue.

Results During 7-Day Promotion

Sales: $7,000

Redemptions: 417

Marketing Ad Spend: $0

Analyzing Your Bottom Line

Before implementing some of these strategies and spending any money on a campaign, you need to do a quick analysis to better understand where marketing dollars will be going. We have reviewed these ideas in other sections, but we repeat them here to ensure that you start with the basics and move forward making educated decisions.

Questions to consider when reviewing your current strategy:

- Can you track your success?
- Do you have concrete assessments or just feelings and guesses?
- Do you have records you can pull out to analyze?
- What do your customers think about the way you engage with them?
- Do you get feedback from them about your ads and/or offers?
- Are your sales up or down? Is that due to marketing or other factors?

With those questions answered, you should be able to determine how you get your best results.

Now move forward:

1. Using your analysis of your current marketing, identify the tactics that are not increasing your revenue and reduce their budget to $0.

2. Replace those old marketing strategies with new marketing strategies (detailed instructions ahead).

Start Small

To start this process, we recommend running a simple paid advertisement to reach locals in your area and building upon that based on your results. This low-budget step will help you gain confidence — even on a tight budget — as you make the transition to this new style of marketing.

You don't need a huge budget to run a successful campaign. Obviously, you want to give yourself a fair shot, but even just $100 can reach upwards of 50,000–100,000 customers on Facebook and Instagram; even a small budget can be enough to build momentum and start producing results. As you gain more confidence in earning a return on your ads, you can slowly increase the budget over time.

The population of the United States is 325 million, 214 million of which are users on Facebook. We can safely assume that two-thirds of your local customers are using Facebook or Instagram daily on their phones.

Demographics can make a difference, so consider your typical customer profile when creating your ads. Just be careful not to write off your ability to reach older age groups on social media. The average Facebook user in the US is over 40 years old and over 60% of seniors (65+) have profiles. Even starting with a small investment, will open you to a great opportunity to reach customers in your local area.

First-time users may find some of the features and automation we use for chat marketing to be a little complicated. Many of the omnichannel reengagement strategies can become a little complex. Therefore, we recommend starting first with just Facebook and/or Instagram ads, and then evolving into a strategy across Messenger, email and SMS. Take it step by step because there is a lot here.

> Start with Facebook and Instagram advertising, and then add on the chat marketing automation strategies as your skills progress.

These skills take time to learn and conquer. This initial investment will pay dividends in the long term and help you stay in front of the competition.

Whether you decide to go at it alone or hire help, in our opinion, the best approach is to at least be knowledgeable about how all of the systems work, even if others end up doing the actual labor.

Get Ready, Get Set, Go!

Now that we've given you an overview, you're ready to set up your first promotion.

Get Ready

The first two decisions you must make:

1. What kind of offer do you want to promote at your restaurant?
2. Who do you want to target?

First - let's decide on your offer. Aggressive offers on social media typically do the best. The more generous the offer, the more likely someone is to take action on it. Put yourself in the shoes of the potential customers -- what would get YOU excited enough to get off of your couch and go visit the restaurant? Feel free to do whatever you like, but our recommendation is to offer something for free or do some type of exciting giveaway. Additionally, make sure you choose an offer that is strong enough to bring in sufficient business to offset the extra food cost.

Below are a few offers that we've seen to produce the best results through social media ads:

- *Buy One Get One Free (on a high-ticket item)*

    This offer tends to create high check values, despite giving a large discount, because guests bring in their friends and family when redeeming the offer and in bringing in multiple guests from one ad, you are essentially saving on the acquisition cost of these new guests. Additionally, this type of offer allows the restaurant to showcase their signature menu items from your restaurant to these first-time guests, which ideally leaves a lasting impression.

- *Free Appetizer (*with any purchase)*

    This offer is pretty self-explanatory but the appetizer you choose for this offer is your key to success. The last thing that you want is for guests to visit, get their free appetizer, and then just leave. When deciding on what kind of appetizer to offer up, choose an item that pairs well with an entrée. For example, many people would like to have a side of fries with a burger or mashed potatoes with a steak but rarely would they want those appetizers alone. Additionally, it's important to add in *with any purchase* to ensure guests to make those larger purchases to go with their free appetizer so you can drive up those check values!

- *Free Low-Selling, Low-Cost Item*

  Many restaurants have food items that taste amazing, but for whatever reason, don't seem to sell. However, once guests try the item, it gives them a reason to order it again the next time they visit with their meal. An example of this kind of offer might be a "free cookie" offer. After experiencing how good of a sweet dessert this is, a customer may be prone to order this again and pay for it on their next visit. Even though this item may not add a ton of profit for the restaurant per purchase, if the customer begins to order it every time when they return, the numbers add up. We look at free, low-selling items as an easy way to stack a guest's order and increase check amounts over time.

Get Set

Next, decide who you want to target by asking yourself the following questions:

- How old are my most ideal customers?
- How far do my customers travel to visit my restaurant?
- Where can I capture their attention?

When running any type of customer acquisition campaign, we see the most success on Facebook and Instagram and so we will address our step by step process by using these platforms. Over time, you may want to look at other platforms or get customers to download your app, or even join a loyalty system. However, as a potential first-time marketer, we recommend you stick to promoting on these popular platforms first!

Back to the promotion, you're designing: You've decided what your offer is going to be like and who you will target. Now it's time to decide how long your promotion will last *and* how many people will be able to use it. It's important to put an expiration date or redemption limitation on the offers you have in order to create a sense of urgency for those seeing the promotion. If you fail to do so, fewer prospects will redeem the offer. Give customers a reason to visit your restaurant within the next couple of days or let them know it's only for a limited number of guests. Phrases such as "Offer expires in 7 days" or "To the next 100 customers" increases the sense of urgency and overall redemption percentage. Whether or not you decide to enforce these rules is up to you, but having some restrictions in the messaging of your marketing is a best practice!

Go!

Before launching your Facebook and Instagram campaigns, you need to prepare:

- A high-resolution picture or video of the food you want to promote
- Ad copy with an attractive, clear and, easily understood offer

Here's an example of ad copy:

GET YOUR FREE [Blank]

The only thing better than one of our [Blank] is TWO!
We'd like to offer you a Buy-One-Get-One-Free [Blank]
on your next visit! ☺

Available for TAKEOUT or DINE IN ONLY. Call us ☺
[Phone Number]

Take a screenshot of this ad and show it to a staff member when you arrive! ☺ *Expires [Expiration Date]*

Launching the Ad

With your Facebook and Instagram ads ready, target locals in close proximity to your restaurant. Use your best judgment in determining how far people will realistically drive to visit you. For more urban areas, go smaller, maybe two to three miles. For more rural areas, it's best to go a little larger, expanding the distance to eight to fifteen miles, or more if you like.

If you have multiple locations, you can type in each address one by one inside Facebook Ads Manager, so you can target each location's specific community with the same message. Facebook's targeting technology is amazing. You can even segment your audience by people who live in the area, people who are commuting to work, or people traveling to the area. The extent of knowledge that Facebook has gathered is kind of scary, but it's very helpful for us as advertisers.

Facebook will give you the option to run ads from your Facebook or Instagram page by "boosting" a post, however, we don't recommend this route. When you advertise from the page level it's easy for the platform to take your marketing dollars and run without providing you with a clear return. Managing all of your campaigns from Ads Manager, no matter how small, will keep your tracking as sharp as possible.

Once you launch the ad, it's time to start recording redemptions. In your restaurant, create a button in your POS system and teach your employees how to track each customer that visits with the offer. At the end of the campaign, check the number (and value) of redemptions accounted for by your POS. This simple step will help you assess if your campaign was profitable and determine how to move forward.

POS Tracking

The example ad we just explained will not integrate directly into your POS system and doesn't use automation to capture unique pieces of customer information, such as a phone number and email. This starter campaign is a simple first step that you can execute to draw customers into your restaurant. As you become more familiar and learn more about the platforms, you can add complexity to your campaigns.

Even if you're not the one building these campaigns, these tips and techniques will give you a baseline understanding. If you want your business to stay competitive in today's market, you must understand how to attract customers through social media.

Case Study: Dish Society

If you are looking to set a new foundation for your digital strategy, you might be similar to our client Dish Society, a growing chain with four locations in the Houston market.

Before working with Misfit Media, this farm-to-table chain had their hands in a number of marketing channels — public relations, mailers, posting to social pages and emails — but nothing seemed to move the needle.

After implementing our acquisition strategy, this restaurant chain filled six or seven additional tables per day, accounting for a 6% increase of overall sales.

By promoting various offers through Facebook and Instagram ads, we had 997 redemptions, while reaching 297,000 people in the Houston area. The best part about this campaign was that 70% of customer redemptions were first-time visits, attracting a completely new customer base. After customers clicked on the ads, we drove them into Facebook Messenger, where we captured their email, phone number and how much they spent.

In this case, instead of waiting around and hoping the traditional forms of media would grow their restaurant, Dish Society went on the offense and added $24,000 to their bottom line in the first sixty days of implementing this new system.

60-Day Stats

Sales: $24,000

Ad Spend: $4,000

Contacts Collected: 5,516

Redemptions: 997

Chapter 7

THE ANATOMY OF A KILLER AD

How to Make a Winning Ad on Social Media

When it comes to running ads on social media, ads with offers are the best way to go. Customers are much more likely to give their contact information, when they receive a promotion or discount in return. The more familiar the prospective customer is with your restaurant brand, the less aggressive an offer you will need to put in front of them to capture their information. Higher value offers will capture the most attention.

In this chapter, we show you how to drive unfamiliar/cold leads into your marketing funnel and then into your business as paying customers.

Ultimately, it's mastering this cold-to-hot conversion that will help any restaurant scale and grow its business.

"A business that cannot drive in new customer traffic on demand is not a business at all."

Brett Linkletter

The world as we know it today is crowded, full of distractions and competitive. To capture the attention of potential new customers, you must be creative, different, and eye-catching. Your ads need to stop people in their social feeds.

Marketing is often defined by "the articulation of what makes a product or service good." However, in order to be effective today, we need more than just a strong message.

When creating an ad on Facebook, there are a number of elements to consider, including:

- The headline — The largest text in your ad, which should state your offer.
- The link description — The smaller text, which goes under the headline.
- The copy — The smaller text, in which you describe what your ad is about or is offering.
- The call-to-action button — The objective you want to achieve from users clicking the ad or button. In this case, and most cases, we are using a "send message" objective to drive customers into a one-on-one chat conversation.
- The creative — Either a photo or video.

Below is an example of an ad we made for one of our sandwich
QSR brands with arrows pointing to each part of the ad:

Instagram ads are similar, but without a headline, as shown below:

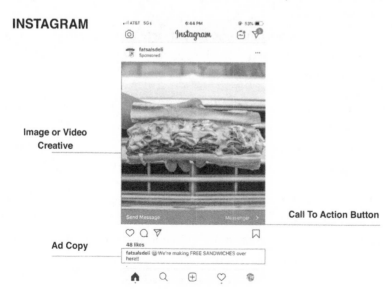

The next concept you must grasp is how a user on Facebook views an ad. When a prospective customer sees your ad on their social media app, their eyes will usually first go to the creative, the photo or video. If the creative catches their attention and stops them from scrolling, they tend to read the headline second, followed by the copy, and then the call-to-action button.

Since the creative is the first thing a potential customer focuses on, it ranks as one of the most important elements in your ads. You must invest the time and effort necessary to make the content attractive, eye-catching, and representative of your brand.

The Creative — Photo or Video?

Facebook gives you the option to use videos or photos on their ad platform. We usually choose photos when it comes to local restaurant marketing.

The reason we usually choose photos over videos is because they are much easier to create. We typically run one campaign per month, so it's important that we get new content out very often. Video production often takes longer than expected and can push back a deadline.

If you have an awesome video team that can help you produce some killer pieces of content, by all means go for it! However, if creating a mouthwatering video proves to be too difficult or takes too much time, don't stress — photos will work just fine.

Always keep in mind that Facebook often changes their algorithms on what they favor, in terms of video or photo content. Social media advertising constantly evolves and it's important to stay up-to-date on current social trends.

What Kind of Photos Should I Use for My Ads?

Restaurant owners often get tripped up and intimidated, when it comes to producing content for their brands. We'd like to preface this by stating that creating stunning photos to market your restaurant is not a difficult task!

Here are some tips for shooting awesome photos:

- Focus on the FOOD

We cannot stress this enough. Your food is your moneymaker, and, therefore, it needs to be the focus of your ads to attract new customers! We also recommend having only one or two items in your photo.

People prefer close-up shots that showcase the item you're promoting. Think of the many photos shared by millennials of what they are eating. Embrace their bragging strategy in your food photography.

You don't need a fancy camera, and you definitely do not need to hire a professional. When it comes to taking photos of your food, your iPhone or Android phone work perfectly! (If you have access to a professional and want some extra nice photos, go for it.) The bottom line is that you can almost always get the same results without a professional photographer.

Taking the Perfect Food Photo

There are a few things you will need:

- Natural lighting
- A solid surface or background

- The best-looking burger, sandwich, pizza, or whatever you want to feature

Natural lighting is *always* better than artificial lighting, especially with mobile phones. Cameras pick up colors and take overall better shots, when the scene is illuminated with natural light.

We recommend setting up your stage near a window on a sunny day. However, avoid direct sunlight to prevent overexposure.

Remember, we want all of the focus of the photo to be the food, so shoot your food photos with a solid background, surface, or tabletop. Avoid extra items on the table or in the background, and stay away from printed, multi-colored surfaces or tablecloths. Items in the background and loud prints can be distracting and detract from your delicious food.

Before you start taking pictures, make sure that your food looks delicious! If it's a burger, make sure you can see all of the layered ingredients. If it's a sandwich, cut it in half so you can see what's inside. If it's a salad, make sure all the ingredients are bright, colorful, and visible. An eye-catching photo will stop the scroll and get a potential customer to read your offer.

Use UGC (User-Generated Content) for Your Ads

One marketing advantage that restaurants have over other businesses, is that customers *love* to take photos of their food (when it looks good) and share them on social media sites, such as Instagram or Facebook, or review pages, like Yelp.

If you are looking for good content, we recommend checking out the photos your restaurant has been tagged in online! Oftentimes, we find that restaurant owners are surprised at the number of amazing photos taken at their restaurants that have already been posted. <u>Caution:</u> Always ask customers for permission, before using their photos in your marketing.

Use Your Most-Liked Content in Your Ads

If you are struggling to decide which photos to use for an ad, look at the photos you've already posted on your social media pages. Whichever photos received the most likes are a good indication of what will perform the best in your ads.

Headline and Copy

Your headline and copy are intended to inform the consumer what your ad is about and what you are offering.

The headline is the second section of a Facebook ad (after the creative visual) that a consumer will see. You only get twenty-five characters for this section, so make sure your headline is short, to the point, and attractive to the viewer.

Since the majority of the ads we run are intended for new customers and because we typically run a decent amount of BOGO offers, we'll use headline copy such as:

- "FREE Pizza!!! ••"
- "FREE Burger!!! ••"
- "Want a FREE Burger?! •"

Using capital letters adds emphasis and directs attention to a word. You should include emojis. They are eye-catching and make the ad a bit more fun.

Since our goal is to get the consumer to click the "Send Message" button in the lower right-hand corner of the ad, we use arrows or pointing fingers that aim to the right. These little tricks will drastically improve your CTR (click-through rate).

The text copy of your ad (the smaller text above or below the ad) is the last section of the ad that customers will read. The copy should clearly describe what you are offering and give instructions on how to accept the offer.

The first line should repeat your headline's offer in a creative way, while making use of capital letters and emojis to direct and grab attention.

In our example with Fat Sal's below, we used:

FREE SANDWICH! (for our headline)

• We're making **FREE SANDWICHES** over here!! (in the first line of the text copy)

Notice how we are repeating the offer for free sandwiches, making use of all caps, emojis, and incorporating the use of the company tagline, "We're making sandwiches over here."

Brett & Jace pictured at Fat Sal's restaurant

The reason to repeat the headline on a Facebook ad is to reaffirm to the consumer that there is an offer and if they continue reading, they'll learn how to get this offer. Keep in mind that **ads on Instagram do not get a headline at all.** This first line in your text copy becomes the first text piece a user on Instagram will read.

Ad Copy

The next section of your text will be the body of your ad copy. In this section, you want to describe in detail exactly how a prospect can claim the offer.

Here's what we wrote for the Fat Sal's ad:

> *Sandwiches are best shared with friends & for a limited time, we're offering TWO sandwiches for the price of one!*
>
> *Click "Send Message" below and we'll send you this FAT offer through Facebook Messenger.*
>
> *You'll be enrolled in our VIP Offers program and be the first to get the best monthly promos!*
>
> *Click "Send Message" below for your BOGO SANDWICH OFFER."*

Let's break this down:

- We introduced the copy with the reason why we are making this BOGO offer, by saying: "Sandwiches are best shared with friends."
- We then created a sense of urgency, by stating "for a limited time."
- Next, we stated the offer with "we're offering TWO sandwiches for the price of one!" so the customer understands exactly what the deal is.

In the next three lines, we instructed the user on how to get the deal.

- "Click 'Send Message' below and we'll send you this FAT offer through Facebook Messenger."

This line incorporates the customer's branding, while also providing details on how the reader will receive their coupon.

- The second-to-last line explains additional perks they will receive by clicking "Send Message."

You want to make sure the user knows you will continue to send them messages, even after the deal is over. Leads should be told that they will continue getting messages, so they are not caught off guard or upset when you send them a message at a later date.

- In the last line, you will typically restate how to get the deal.

A/B TESTING YOUR ADS

Now that you have the foundation for what you will write in your ads and the creative elements you will use, the next aspect you want to think about is A/B testing.

A/B Testing is defined by Optimizely.com as:

> "An experiment where two or more variants of an ad are shown to users at random, and statistical analysis is used to determine which variation performs better for a given conversion goal."

Always test at least a couple variations for any ad or offer you create to ensure you get the best results possible. Tracking your results and measuring your success helps make the decision process clear.

For testing purposes, we recommend choosing one good headline, writing two text copies, and using two different creative elements. This will give you a total of four variations of your ad for testing. You are welcome to test more variations, but this is a good place to start with a low advertising budget.

After running your ads for a few days, Facebook will automatically choose the top performer and scale your budget on that winning ad.

Case Study: 5 Napkin Burger

5 Napkin Burger in New York City is an excellent example of implementing this digital attraction method. We are proud to have our second official Facebook Case Study published with 5 Napkin Burger: www.facebook.com/business/success/5-napkin-burger

There are several ways to get prospects into your marketing system. All of the methods open up a one-on-one chat feature, which helps create more meaningful relationships with your prospects. However, in our experience, we see the promotions with high value offers work the most effectively across any restaurant concept.

The campaign for 5 Napkin Burger, which ran from December 11, 2018, through January 31, 2019, helped the restaurant connect with an entirely new segment of prospective customers and tracked the exact revenue of the campaign.

Prior to working with us, 5 Napkin relied on organic social media postings, influencer marketing, and other traditional outreach methods. Those methods were helpful, but the company struggled to measure the impact of its marketing, so it partnered with our team to find a solution.

The famous burger chain is located in the heart of New York City. When we first strategized for this campaign, we knew the densely populated area would pose a challenge. The burger chain has numerous competitors in the surrounding area. We decided that our best chance at driving sales was by targeting people who lived in Manhattan and people who commuted to and worked on the island. We targeted both of these audiences using geo-targeting on their mobile phones.

After we narrowed down our targeting, we needed a killer offer that would get people excited. We decided to run their best-selling item — burgers — as a promotional deal through Facebook and Instagram

ads. While the promotion did come with food costs, we knew that these first-time customers would come back because of the quality of the food and their close proximity to the restaurant's four locations. We also captured these customers' contact info for future remarketing.

A big mistake we see many restaurants make when they spend money on Facebook and Instagram advertising is they forget that many people who see these ads are being reached for the first time and have no idea who they are. At the first touch point, there is no existing brand trust. Just showing someone a picture of your food or an underwhelming deal isn't going to get them to visit your restaurant over their favorite spots.

If you are worried about attracting "deal hunters," remember you don't need to offer customers a deal every time they visit your restaurant. However, if you want to win over a large new segment of customers using social media advertising, we highly recommend presenting them with an offer they can't refuse.

Once we had the creative content and language for the ads, it was time to launch the campaign. Using Facebook Ads Manager, we ran ads that clicked through to Messenger, showcasing the restaurant's best-selling burgers to an audience surrounding its four Manhattan locations. The ads offered two-for-one burgers with a "Send Message" call-to-action button that linked to Messenger. Inside Messenger, 5 Napkin Burger asked people to enter their email address, in exchange for the offer. Again, the key in this campaign was to drive them into Facebook Messenger. This allowed us to capture their information and track how much they spent when they visited the restaurant.

Immediately after launching the campaign, results were off to a slow start. However, we remained patient, knowing that it takes a little time for a campaign to hit full speed. Slowly but surely, redemptions ramped up, and at the two-week mark, 5 Napkin was seeing significant results.

At the 45-day mark, we tracked 417 redemptions from the promotion and captured 2,500 customer contacts. You would think that the average check value would go down because we were offering a discount, but the result was quite the opposite. It went up 20%! Because of the buy-one-get-one-free offer on the burgers, many customers brought in larger parties, introducing an even broader audience to the brand.

45-Day Stats

Sales: $24,039

Ad Spend: $1,500

Contacts Collected: 2,500

Redemptions: 417

After getting this wave of new customers in the door for a first visit, 5 Napkin continued building its relationship, by sending emails and direct messages to people through Facebook Messenger, inviting them to receive relevant restaurant news, specials, and promotions. This continuous line of communication ultimately led to repeat business.

We can't stress enough the importance of learning how to write and create compelling ads. We've covered the ins and outs of creating killer ads on Facebook and Instagram in this chapter. You now have all the tools you need to start creating your own!

Chapter 8

CAMPAIGNS THAT CRUSH

Build, Contest, Birthday, Broadcast, Review Generation

With your newfound knowledge of all these modern marketing elements, it's now time to learn about campaigns that we run for our clients and the specifics behind the magic. We'll teach you how to build a handful of our favorite (and most effective) campaigns.

The types of campaigns which will be explained in this chapter are:

- Build
- Contest
- Birthday
- Broadcast
- Review Generation

Build

The first style of a campaign we run is called a Build campaign. Build campaigns are designed to reach new customers in your area while simultaneously growing a database of fans that we can re-market to. These campaigns are by far the most popular amongst our clientele and where we typically see the best results.

Here's how they work:

At the top of our funnel, the "awareness" stage, we'll start by creating an ad on Facebook and Instagram and adjust our targeting to a few miles or more around the restaurant location. These ads are intended to reach new customers for the restaurant and so we'll need a lead magnet, or an offer in order to incentivize these new potential fans to stop scrolling in their social media newsfeeds and click. Typically for Build campaigns, we'll use a fairly aggressive offer like a BOGO deal, as shown in this example.

As soon as someone clicks to get the offer, we ask to collect the leads: first name, last name, email, phone number, and subscription to Facebook Messenger in exchange for the offer. It's a simple trade: "We'll give you this offer, in exchange for your information!"

From our experience, we've seen that ~80-90% of people who click on these ads are also willing to give up their personal information! However, keep in mind that these numbers are dependent on the quality of the leads and the kind of offer you made to them. A quick note here and another friendly reminder - the more generous the offer, the lower your cost per lead will be!

So, with this new customer lead information, we've now gained the ability to communicate with these leads - but more importantly, these potential customers now have the ability to redeem their offer - for takeout, delivery, or in-store.

Within Manychat, you can set up systems that allow customers to redeem offers or coupons through Messenger.

In order to create an in-store redemption coupon inside Messenger, simply create an automated message that is sent to the customer after they input their personal contact information. In this message, you'll want it to contain a picture and/or graphic that represents the promotion along with a button under it that says "redeem". To redeem an offer, customers can press the button in messenger at the time of visiting the restaurant and show your staff for proof.

After a customer has redeemed the offer through Messenger, fire off another automated message that asks how much the customer spent on their visit. Your customers should then type in their check value, through the messenger chat. We typically see ~5-10% of customers who redeem their offer will want to ignore this step and not enter the check value. In this case, we have formulas and automations set up that will take the last 10 check values and automatically input the average of them for that empty cell. In doing so, we can make sure that there is always at least an average check value for every missed entry!

Lastly, with all this data collected through messenger, it's important to have a method by which you can easily view and understand the data. Using Manychat in combination with a software called Zapier, we have the ability to display all of our data in Google spreadsheets where we can easily track how our campaigns are performing by customer spend, total redemptions, Promo ID's, etc. We'll discuss a bit more on Zapier in the next chapter.

Google Sheets:

Price	Redeem Date	Promo ID
28	12/24/19 7:26 AM	Happy Hour - $4 Drink
58	12/24/19 3:57 PM	Free Onion Rings
72.95	12/25/19 4:03 PM	Free Onion Rings
46.82	12/26/19 11:23 AM	BOGO Burger
18	12/28/19 6:05 AM	Free Onion Rings

In addition to in-store redemptions, you can also set up online redemptions. If you have a direct website link where customers can order online from your restaurant, we highly recommend you leverage Messenger and this marketing funnel to drive more traffic there!

To enable online redemptions for customers, simply add in a button within your messenger flow that allows the customer to choose if they want to redeem an offer *In-store* or *Online*. If a customer clicks Online, drive them to your restaurant's online menu link and then send them a code to use when placing an order to receive the deal. It's that simple!

To set general benchmarks on these campaigns, you'll want to aim for customer leads of around $1 – $2. This means that for every

$1 – $2 you spend on your ad campaign, someone should click on an ad and you will capture their information.

The beauty of this system described here is that it's all trackable, meaning we can see where the customer is in our funnel. We can see whether a customer lead just clicked our ad, or put in their info, or made a purchase or not. Having the tools to see and measure this gives us the ability to follow up with each customer accordingly in a customized manner!

With this system set up correctly, you will finally have clarity on how your marketing is performing and that is powerful.

Not everyone who clicks on these ads will make a purchase at your restaurant in-store or online. In fact, many of our leads may never come in at all. In order to convert the most amount of leads into buyers, we recommend setting up automations that remind customers to come in once they've opted into our database. The amount of remarketing messages you may want to send to a lead is dependent on your preference but we recommend doing at least two reminders.

With these reminder sequences, you will easily be able to drive a second and even third wave of new customers off of the initial campaign. Sending follow-up emails and text messages to remind your leads to visit or order online will typically increase your redemption by another 15–35%!

Again as we described earlier, to really push it to the next level, create restricted deadlines and limitations that will ensure redemption percentages stay high.

If you develop a Build campaign correctly, you should strive to have a customer acquisition cost of $4–$10! Imagine that for every $4 you spent on ads, you could receive a new customer order!

Birthday Campaigns

Birthday campaigns are another way to immediately add an easy bump to your bottom line every single month. These campaigns can run 365 days a year and not see any decrease in performance because you can leverage stored customer information obtained from Facebook and Instagram.

If you remember when you first created your Facebook profile you entered your birthday. This allows advertisers to serve the right promotions leading up to the exact week of someone's birthday. This advertising capability is a low-hanging fruit that many restaurants ignore.

Similar to the Build campaign, an attractive offer is the first step to a successful birthday campaign. Without a good offer, you don't give guests a reason to rally their friends and family to celebrate their birthday at your restaurant. Birthday campaigns can be extremely profitable, because birthday celebrations tend to bring in the highest average check amounts across all types of campaigns. If your restaurant serves alcohol, these promotions are extra effective. People love to celebrate with a round or two, and it's well-known that alcohol not only significantly raises the party's check, but also has larger margins. Most people do not want to spend their birthday alone, so multi-person parties can be expected for any birthday offer.

When building the actual campaign, use Facebook Ads Manager's detailed targeting feature to hyper-target people who have birthdays in the upcoming week. The rest of your campaign set-up is nearly identical to your Build campaign.

From here, you want to drive people into Facebook Messenger to collect more information for your database. Birthday campaigns bring in such high check values, that it is worth running these campaigns to your existing customers through text and email offers all year round.

As with all of your campaigns, you want to capture customers' phone numbers, email addresses, and subscriber information through Facebook Messenger. You should also put a seven-day restriction on the offer to create a sense of urgency and get people to redeem the offer the same week. Throughout the week, send text and email reminders letting people know that their offer is about to expire. By doing so, you are able to get birthday offers claimed for about $1.50–$2.00 and redemption rates of about 20–25%.

By running this type of campaign, you can expect customer acquisition cost to be around $6–$10. For spending $100 a month on advertising, our clients tend to add an extra twenty to thirty birthday visits on a monthly basis using this formula.

Not bad for a $100 investment!

Contest Campaigns

Contest campaigns are a fun way to reach out to new customers or re-engage with an existing database. Unfortunately, many contests run by restaurants may appear fun and exciting, but often are not properly constructed for the restaurant to actually generate sales.

There are many different ways to construct your contest campaign, but we will give you a simple and straightforward method that can be applied to any restaurant.

How it works:

We previously discussed different entry points to draw potential customers into a marketing funnel and into Facebook Messenger. These entry points, as a reminder to you, are QR Codes, URL's, and Ads.

However, if you have a good following on social media, you can easily leverage your followers and direct them into opting in for a contest on Messenger!

The goal is to create a post through your social media that highlights a contest. When someone comments on this post to enter the contest you can automatically send them a message through Messenger.

The trick to making these campaigns profitable is to link an offer to the contest, so everyone who participates has a reason to visit the restaurant to redeem an offer. Again, you can simply post this offer for your followers on your Facebook page to see or if you want to add some extra juice to it, feel free to promote the post with ad dollars and see it go further!

So now that you have the foundation of how this works let's talk about what copy, creative, and contest you will create.

Here's an easy one:

Find a decent-sized jar around the restaurant and fill it with something relevant to the restaurant. This could be mints, buttons, candy, or really anything that allows people to place their guess on how many of that item are in the jar. Take a picture of that jar – this is what you will use for the creative on your post.

Choose a wild prize (offer) that will be sure to generate buzz, like a $100 gift card or "Free Pizza for a Year."

Next, create the post with the creative and copy explaining how customers can enter the contest and win.

Here's a general formula for constructing the right language:

GIVEAWAY TIME

Want to win a [*Insert Giveaway Offer*] ?!

You heard that right! We're giving away a [*Insert Giveaway Offer*] to not one, but TWO lucky winners who can guess how many pins are in the jar below.

Here's how to enter:

1. Comment below how many pins you think are in the jar and you'll be subscribed to our VIP List.
2. Tag a friend.

Every participant will receive a [*Participation Offer*] just for entering!

GOOD LUCK! Mark your calendars; we'll be announcing the winners next month.

Here are a few examples of photos that would work for this campaign:

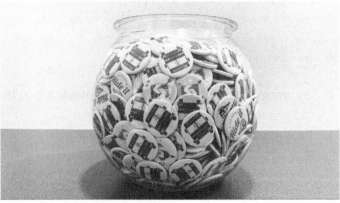

All customers who enter the contest are sent a follow-up promotion via Facebook Messenger, with an offer they can redeem at the restaurant over the next two weeks. As mentioned in the Build and Birthday campaign examples, a better offer will lead to more customers redeeming at your restaurant.

Before customers receive their participation offer, prompt them for their email and phone number, if you don't already have that contact information.

Results from contest campaigns vary based on your restaurant's follower count on Facebook or the amount you are willing to spend on the campaigns. Facebook pages with 5,000+ followers can see an extra $2,000–$3,000 generated from this campaign per location.

If you already have a decent following on your social pages, we recommend giving the contest-style campaign a try for a quick uptick in sales with little to no advertising costs.

Broadcasts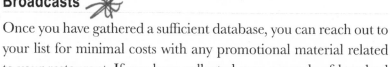

Once you have gathered a sufficient database, you can reach out to your list for minimal costs with any promotional material related to your restaurant. If you have collected even a couple of hundred customers into your database, you are ready to start messaging them on a regular basis to drive sales.

To successfully message your database, it's imperative that you understand the rules and costs associated with each database entry, so you can earn an ROI on your broadcast messages. If you need a refresher on the rules and regulations of each, refer back to the 24-hour rule in Chapter 4.

While not every text message or email blast needs to go back into Facebook Messenger, we do recommend frequently pushing traffic back into the app to track redemptions and create as many one-on-one chats as possible.

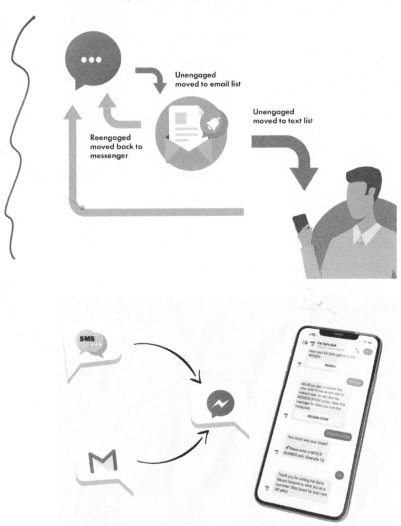

Let's say after running two months of Build Campaigns, you have generated a list of 2,000 phone numbers and emails. This month, you're launching a new happy hour menu, and you'd like to incentivize customers to visit, by offering a free appetizer with any purchase. Your total costs for this hypothetical campaign would be $20 to text all 2,000 people–$.01 per text message. Now one thing to note is that the texts that we send on ManyChat are limited to 160 characters, so you will need to be concise and specific with what you have in your message.

A simple, effective example is shown below for your reference:

New Happy Hour Menu Launch

Visit us between 4–7 pm this week for a Free Appetizer!

Now don't forget, in running your Build Campaign, you've also acquired 2,000 customer emails! You could choose to utilize this email list in addition to or in substitution of your phone list.

However, as we mentioned earlier in our book, each communication channel requires a slightly different method or tone or communication.

The benefit of an email as your communication channel is that you can provide more details about the promotion since we have fewer restrictions on the number of characters that can be on an email. Additionally, you could also include a photo of the food item you are promoting, an address for your restaurant, or even contact information to book a reservation.

Now when it comes to either communication channel, text, or email, you will want to be able to track redemptions from this offer.

In order to do so, simply attach a URL link to both the text and the email to drive customers into Facebook Messenger to redeem the offer.

Using broadcasts effectively and consistently could easily generate thousands in revenue each month for your restaurant over time. Why not make a typically slow time at your restaurant the new busiest time with the newfound power of a broadcast!

Review Generation and Customer Feedback

There's no question that reviews influence customers' trust and decision-making process when visiting your restaurant. If your restaurant has an average rating of 3/5 stars or below, you will most likely get swallowed up by your local competition. Reviews are everything! So how can you use our strategies to help grow your positive 5-star reviews? It's actually very simple – you can add an automation trigger that links customers to your Google and Yelp profiles as a follow up when guests dine with you and redeem an offer. This automation can be added to any of the campaigns above to instantly boost reviews and gather customer feedback. Additionally, we've seen that guests are more likely to leave a review when they've also received a killer offer from a restaurant so this simple addition could lead to a massive lift in positivity for your restaurant!

Again, we recommend you use ManyChat to set this up and drive customers to your desired pages.

Below is an example of a review generator we created using ManyChat:

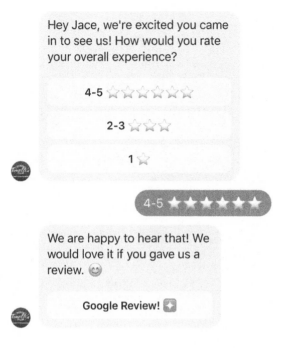

If the feedback is positive, you can drive that customer to a link to access your review pages. If the feedback is negative, you can follow up with the customer to see where you fell short of excellence in hopes to earn that customer back.

The review-generation campaign can be executed in a number of different ways. Depending on your goals or the feedback generated from your customers, you can set this up in several different ways. What we have presented is merely one example of review generation and we will dive into more detail on this in the next chapter!

There you have it! You now know five easy and effective campaigns that are trackable and can be executed by any type of restaurant.

Chapter 9

UNLOCKING THE POWER OF AUTOMATION

In the previous chapter, we showed you some examples of our most popular marketing campaigns that produce customers on demand for restaurants. We've sprinkled the term "automation" throughout this book to break down the fundamentals of automation, especially as it relates to restaurant marketing.

By simple definition, marketing automation is creating a sequence of events that help make a process more efficient and create a better user experience. This can be done in a number of ways. Whether it's improving the ability to attract new guests to your restaurant or increasing operational efficiency, it's an extremely powerful tool when used correctly. Automation allows us as marketers and business owners to do so much more than we would be able to otherwise without it.

Here are some of the key places in your marketing strategy where you can and should use automation:

- **Messages in Messenger -** All of the messages within the Messenger marketing funnel are fully automated but still have a conversational, personal feel.

- **Facebook Ads** - Facebook looks for new customers through a completely automated process. Once you set up your campaign parameters, the inbound lead generation no longer needs human interaction or instruction.

- **Review Generation** - The additional push for people to generate a Google or Yelp review after they check out at the restaurant is fully automated.

Really, there are unlimited strings of digital actions that can either create a better experience for the customers or help the restaurant operate more efficiently.

The biggest benefit of marketing automation is the amount of time you save, especially when thousands of customers are having a one-on-one conversation with your restaurant at any given time. Think about the customer support team that you would need to physically go through and nurture each conversation. The responses wouldn't be possible without automation.

As we previously mentioned, another significant benefit of automation is giving guests a consistent, better experience. An automated response can give someone what they want faster than if a human were involved. If a guest needs access to a promotional coupon, an automated response can deliver the coupon instantaneously; versus taking time out of someone's day to call the restaurant or talk to a support team member.

When looking at this new age of marketing, we utilize Facebook and Instagram to connect with new customers with the intention of getting them to spend their personal time at a restaurant. A large reason the strategies we discuss in this book work is because of the automation and the follow-up process. A reason many traditional forms of marketing don't work as well anymore is that there is no follow-up process. As the saying goes, "The fortune is in the follow-up." Automating your marketing funnel not only guarantees that each lead will receive a follow-up, but also reduces your need for human involvement.

We rarely see any action taken on the first touch point between our clients and the prospective customers they are trying to reach. With marketing automation attached to a campaign, you immediately become intertwined with the specific actions your prospects take. You can then follow up through email, text message, or Facebook Messenger to remind customers to redeem the offer you originally messaged to them.

With basic marketing automation strapped to any campaign, you can typically see a three to five time increase in overall redemptions. In any Facebook campaign, you may see 3% of customers redeem an offer, but with the right automation systems, you will see up to 35% of customers redeem the promotions they received through social media.

We'd like to introduce the concept of the "Straight Track Method." This system is a core element in our approach to any marketing campaign. The principle behind the Straight Track Method (STM) is keeping prospective customers on a linear path. We live in a world where content and marketing are put in front of our faces 24/7. It is extremely easy for people to get distracted. Although someone might have had the intention of visiting your restaurant, life gets in the way and they forget. They fall off the "track" to visit your restaurant. Therefore, your job is to keep prospects on the right track to visit the restaurant. In order to keep them on track, you need to apply automation to remind them to come visit you.

For example, imagine you are doing a promotion for buy-one-get-one-Free burger with a 30-day expiration date on it. Without any automation in place, you don't have any safety nets to keep the recipients from forgetting about your offer. However, after applying STM, you now have a simple, yet powerful system to move your redemption percentage from 3 – 15% and onwards to 35%.

If you apply automation using STM to your 30-day offer, here's what it might look like:

In this example, we'd be following up three times through email and twice through text messaging. If at any time a guest visits the restaurant, we would immediately pull them out of the sequence of reminder messages. With these five follow-up steps, results are likely to double or even triple. The language should also be kept congruent throughout the five messages so each message builds on the prior.

Day 1 (Email)   "Here's the Buy-One-Get-One-Free Burger you requested."

Day 8 (Email)   "Remember this offer has a 30-day expiration date."

Day 14 (Text)   "The redemption window is halfway complete — 2 weeks remaining."

Day 20 (Email) "Only 10 days left" ☺

Day 30 (Text)   "Today is the final day. We'll see you soon!"

Remember, customers originally asked for this offer. They can choose to opt out of reminders at any time. Guests appreciate these messages to help remind them that their offer is still available.

You can get even more value from your original campaign, by turning redemptions through Messenger into direct customer feedback, as we explained in the last chapter with review generation, or inviting customers to an already existing loyalty program. The possibilities are truly endless.

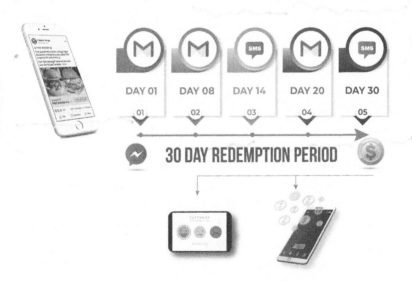

In this case, take the same marketing automation that you created above, but for every person who redeems an offer, move them through additional steps to get even more value from the guest.

Two hours after a guest leaves the restaurant after redeeming their offer, we can automatically set up our campaign, to send a follow-up message through text or Messenger saying something like:

> "Hey, [First Name], we hope you had a great meal. We're always trying to improve our business and your feedback helps us serve you better! Are you open to taking a quick survey to let us know about your experience?"

Messages sent via text or Messenger typically have an open rate of 80-98% so we can guarantee that nearly every guest sees this message. Out of the total number of recipients, we see about one-third of all people leave feedback, which helps our restaurant clients improve their business. This is an automated way to collect real-time feedback while simultaneously driving sales.

If you are serious about using these marketing systems to actually turn a profit in your restaurant business, the Straight Track Method shouldn't be treated as a suggestion. It's absolutely mandatory to learn these principles and start applying them to your business.

According to Statistica.com, in the United States alone, mobile phone usage increases every year, and 81% of Americans now have smartphones, an increase from 35% back in 2011. Cell phone screen time usage has increased to three hours and thirty minutes every day in 2019 for the average American! You can sleep well at night knowing the time you're investing to learn the platforms where your customers are spending the most of their time will pay dividends.

Again, we use primarily ManyChat when it comes to setting up the majority of our automation for our marketing campaigns but in addition to this software, and when it comes to setting up more advanced features to collect in-depth feedback from our customers, another software we recommend using is called "Typeform" (Typeform.com).

We love Typeform for its slick user interface, plug and play features, and its ability to neatly embed into Messenger. Through Typeform, you can set up customized questions that you can have your guest fill out after their visit such as:

1. How likely are you to recommend us to a friend on a scale of 1-10?
2. What other items would you like to see on our menu?
3. Do you have any comments or feedback on your recent experience with us?

The great part about Typeform is the format in which we can ask guests questions. We can set up questions that can be answered with options "A B C or D" or we can set up questions that are completely open-ended. Being able to customize our questions like so and getting this kind of in-depth feedback is incredible!

The questions answered will appear in your account within Typeform but if you want an easy way to automate where they all appear for you/your employees to be able to see as well, we recommend you check out another software we utilize, which is called "Zapier" (Zapier.com).

You can think of Zapier as a "glue" that links software to other software. One example would be using Zapier to export data collected in Typeform into a Google Sheet of your choice so that you can simply view that data in Google Sheets. In doing so, you wouldn't have to give someone your Typeform account login to view the data but could send them a link to your Google Sheet.

Another example would be to use Zapier as a tool for tracking customer transactions and exporting data received inside Facebook Messenger (email, phone number, birthday, etc.). If you were to set up this automation so that your sales data were exported to the same sheet as your feedback survey from Typeform, you could easily track your sales as well as the feedback that came through on one sheet!

This is exactly what we did with a client of ours based out of Los Angeles.

Case Study: Gathering Feedback

Before we jump into this next case study, we want to preface it by saying *all* of our clients use automation in their marketing campaigns. As you have learned in this chapter, automation is an incredibly powerful tool, when used correctly.

While our services primarily focus on driving revenue for our clients, another powerful method where automation can be used is to collect customer feedback.

Most restaurants attempt to collect feedback from customers. However, we typically see little strategy built around our clients' feedback systems. Most services on the market today do not provide an ability to seamlessly collect feedback from guests to learn more about their dine-in experience. Responses are often collected days after a guest visits the restaurant, usually in an email format saying, "Let us know about your experience!" Sending an email with a header like this usually results in low participation numbers.

We've constructed a guest feedback system that happens through a one-on-one chat experience on the guest's phone.

Our clients are usually curious to learn a few key insights that will help them make better choices. In late 2018, we began working with a German sausage restaurant here in Los Angeles. They wanted to leverage the guest feedback system to its fullest potential. We set up simple automation that followed up with guests two hours after they redeemed the offer at the restaurant.

The additional automation came in through the customer's expenditure entry. Once someone entered their check value, a two-hour timer started. When the timer went off, they received a direct message asking about their experience. We created a list of questions through Typeform that wanted to ask the guest and we received 501 surveys out of a total of 1,212 guest redemptions! This means that more than 1 in 3 customers gave us feedback on their experience.

We asked the following questions in our survey:

1. Did we meet your expectations? (Yes, No)
2. How likely are you to recommend us to a friend? (1-5 scale)
3. Do you have any other comments on your experience that you could provide us with? (open-ended answers were received)

Based on the surveys we received, we saw an average rating of 4.7/5, which was incredible for our client to see. Additionally, we received insights on which dishes customers like best and why, details on the friendliness of staff, etc. These insights helped us as marketers understand what gets the customers excited while also helping our clients collect feedback so they can better their business overall and make more strategic decisions moving forward.

Campaign results over 3 months across 2 locations:

Ad Spend: $3,000

Revenue Gained: $26,000

Redemptions: 1,212

Customer Surveys Collected: 501

As you can see, not only was this campaign able to drive a substantial amount of revenue, but we also gained significant insight into the customer's dining experience!

Chapter 10

THE CAMPAIGN STACKING METHOD

In the last chapter, we covered the most effective places in your campaigns to implement automation. This chapter is all about how to compound your results month over month.

There's something special that occurs once we launch a series of campaigns. When this happens, the campaigns begin to stack on top of one another, which is how our clients see insane results from their marketing efforts.

In the previous chapter, we gave the example of running a buy-one-get-one-free burger offer. With automation attached to this offer, any restaurant can see an immediate influx of customers. Let's say the client runs the campaign for thirty days — that's only one month's campaign. However, if they are launching these campaigns on a monthly basis, they can expect that these results will build on one another.

Once your database begins to grow, you can start to leverage the Campaign Stacking Method. As long as you are consistent with running campaigns, this will create a snowball effect and build on itself over time.

The Campaign Stacking Method has three main elements:

1. Use Facebook and Instagram ads to target locals within close proximity of your restaurant, depending on the surrounding area.

2. Generate a database of these local customers using Facebook Messenger, text, and email.

3. Monetize the database consistently to actually track customer spend at the restaurant.

ACQUISITION MARKETING

5 MILES

STACKING METHOD

Let's say in Month 1, you run a BOGO burger offer and you get 1,000 customers into your database. Obviously, not every person who claims the offer online will visit the restaurant. However, after applying a basic automation to remind guests to redeem their offer, you may see that you can at least 10% of people to visit the restaurant. So 100 (1,000 x 10%) people visit in the first 30 days and you are left with 900 people who did not visit.

During Month 2, run a similar campaign and get another 1,000 people to claim another offer. Let's say this time you run a free appetizer offer and, of course, still collect prospective guests' information to add to the database. If you apply the exact same strategy, you get 100 people to claim the offer within 30 days.

But wait! Remember, you have 900 people from the previous month who did not claim the offer. So, then you decide to apply the Straight Track Method and re-engage with these guests and in doing so you should send this group a text message that says:

"Hey <first name>, we noticed that you received an offer from us last month. Would you like us to extend the offer another 30 days?"

From this text message, you get another 10% of the Month 1 leads to visit the restaurant. 900 x 10% = 90.

So, what is beginning to happen here? In Month 2, you got 100 new people to visit the restaurant for a free appetizer, and you had 90 prospects from Month 1 redeem the offer they initially didn't use, which brings you to a total of 190 redemptions in Month 2! Your campaign from Month 1 "stacked" on top of your campaign from Month 2 will generate even more sales.

At the end of Month 2, your redemption percentage from Month 1 moved from 10% to 19%.

If you ran a birthday campaign for Month 3, you might offer a free entree. Once again, you will project that you are able to get 1,000 people in the local area who have a birthday that month to claim an offer, while you collect their email, cell phone, and subscriber info on Facebook Messenger. From the 1,000 people, you are able to get 10% of those people to visit, which equals another 100 guests.

	Month 1	Month 2
Month 1 1000 Database Entries	100	90
Month 2 1000 Database Entries		100
Month 3 1000 Database Entries		
Total Restaurant Visits	100	190

In addition to the 100 redemptions from the birthday offer in Month 3, you also have 900 people in your database from Month 2 and 810 people in your database from Month 1. Send both groups another text message that reminds them to visit the restaurant to redeem an outstanding offer. In Month 3, you then get another 5% of guests from Month 1 (810 x 5% = 40.5) and another 10% of guests from Month 2 (900 x 10%).

How the results stack up for Month 3:

	Month 1	Month 2	Month 3
Month 1 1000 Database Entries	100	90	40
Month 2 1000 Database Entries		100	90
Month 3 1000 Database Entries			100
Total Restaurant Visits	100	190	230

You can see that your efforts from running consistent campaigns are paying off as you still see redemptions flowing through from Months 1 and 2, while Month 3 brings in 230 redemptions. Now you're really starting to roll.

However, it keeps getting better.

Remember, over the course of three months you have grown your list by 1,000 people every single month, now totaling over 3,000 contacts. These are people you can message for any upcoming promotion for $.01 per message.

Do you think if you sent 3,000 people a text about a new happy hour special, you would be able to generate interest from at least 2–3% of them? If so, that would be an additional 60–90 guests on top of the people claiming offers from their initial offer online. How about spending $30 to get 60–90 transactions at your restaurant? We'd take the trade every time.

What's amazing about these campaigns is they are almost completely automated, with zero to little human maintenance involved. It's a well-oiled machine that brings you customers on demand.

The Campaign Stacking Method sits as a staple of every campaign we execute for our clients at Misfit Media, which is why our clients and customers can see tangible results in a short period of time, all while building a database of guests to generate future revenue.

Chapter 11

LET'S GET THIS PARTY STARTED

"Knowledge is power: You hear it all the time, but knowledge is not power. It's only potential power. It only becomes power when we apply it and use it. Somebody who reads a book and doesn't apply it, they're at no advantage over someone who's illiterate. None of it works unless YOU work. We have to do our part. If knowing is half the battle, action is the second half of the battle."

Jim Kwik

In this book, you've learned a number of new principles:

- Don't ever settle for the status quo! What most people are doing isn't always the right thing or the best option.

- Likes and follows on social media don't mean butts in the seats at your restaurants. Social engagement is only a small segment of social media and oftentimes doesn't even lead to success in sales.

- When it comes to this new age of marketing, everything is measurable. Seek to understand your wins, losses, and learnings.

In short, you've learned how to market your restaurant like a true Misfit.

Ultimately, with these newly equipped skills, you will see your marketing ROI down to the dollar, so you can continue investing in your business, knowing with confidence that you are making the right decisions to grow.

We have provided the resources and knowledge needed to start driving new guests into your restaurant immediately. Go ahead and take a stab at your first campaign! The best way to learn is through experience.

We recommend applying the principles outlined in this book as soon as possible. Whether you are trying to learn how to execute this new style of marketing yourself or looking for a strategic partner, don't put it off. Try our methods while the concepts are fresh in your mind. These methods work for every type of restaurant from mom and pops to bigger corporate chains, and we are certain they will work for you.

However, we want to make it clear that these marketing strategies are not the silver bullet to saving a restaurant on its last legs. A fancy marketing campaign won't save your business if you don't have everything else in order at your restaurant such as delicious food and outstanding service for your guests.

When launching any of our marketing campaigns, we expect to reach tens of thousands or hundreds of thousands of people every single time. However, if you reach this many people, you'd want to have your business set up and ready to be able to delight those who come in as a result of the marketing, right?

We often tell our clients that our marketing programs will "accelerate the truth" of their brand, for better or worse. Our strategies will get more people to know about a restaurant, enjoy a restaurant, and ultimately talk about that restaurant fairly quickly. Remember – first impressions are so key in this line of business. A first-time bad experience could turn off a customer from ever coming back.

It doesn't matter how damn great your marketing is if when customers come in they don't like your food and leave uneasy about the service.

However, if your restaurant has an amazing reputation, people love your product, and guests can't help but say great things about you, then you're set up for success and ready to utilize our strategies.

Overall, the restaurant industry is an exciting place to be today because the business landscape is changing drastically. There's much to learn as new technologies and challenges emerge.

And you know what we would say:

Why not become the first one in your area with this system?

Why not become the next 100+ location chain?

More than anything, this promotional edge will give your business clarity on how your marketing efforts are actually performing. Our entire marketing philosophy comes down to accurately tracking and improving results. Our message to you is the same message we tell our clients: once you see the benefits and gain some confidence after seeing an ROI from a campaign listed in this book, you're going to be hooked.

Many restaurant owners dream about sharing their food and experiences with as many people as possible. Adopting the Misfit mindset and applying our marketing principles will help you succeed in your endeavors.

We hope our strategies will help your business grow financially but more importantly we hope that by doing so it will allow you to spend more time doing the things you love, whether that's spending more time with your family and friends or opening up new locations.

When applied correctly, our strategies can create more meaningful relationships between your brand and your most optimal customers 24/7.

That's not an exaggeration. It's the truth.

So what are you waiting for? Go get after it and remember – Change is not an option; it is a requirement. So make the change, put in the work, and reap the benefits of marketing your restaurant like a Misfit.

CONTACTING US

Want to speak with the Misfits about your restaurant? If you're interested in discussing opportunities to work directly with our team, visit our website at www.misfitmedia.com and book a call with us! You will be paired up with an expert on our team who will take the time to learn more about your restaurant and determine whether there is a good fit. Be sure to mention on the call that you read our book!

Our Appreciation for Those Who Helped Us

We want to thank all of our clients, especially those early on, who put their trust in us, believed in us, and allowed us to put forth our best efforts to help grow their restaurants through our unique marketing strategies! We are very grateful for where we are today and remain forever humble, as we continue to succeed.

For those who read this book, we hope you can see our dedication to helping restaurant business owners navigate the ever-changing industry. We truly care about our clients and the results we help them achieve. Above all, we love helping business owners succeed. Your success fuels us every day to continue making an impact on people's lives and continue onward to achieve our goals.

Thank you very much for reading, and we wish you success.

Sincerely,
Brett & Jace

Made in United States
Orlando, FL
29 April 2023